50 Premium Island Recipes for Home

By: Kelly Johnson

Table of Contents

- Coconut Crusted Mahi Mahi
- Pineapple Teriyaki Chicken Skewers
- Mango Salsa with Tortilla Chips
- Island Style BBQ Ribs
- Caribbean Jerk Shrimp
- Ahi Tuna Poke Bowl
- Tropical Fruit Salad
- Jamaican Jerk Chicken
- Pineapple Coconut Rice
- Spicy Papaya Salsa
- Grilled Lobster with Garlic Butter
- Key Lime Pie
- Coconut Curry Fish Stew
- Rum Punch
- Pineapple Ginger Glazed Ham
- Coconut Lime Chicken
- Bahamian Conch Fritters
- Grilled Pineapple with Cinnamon Sugar
- Guava BBQ Sauce
- Caribbean Spiced Pork Tenderloin
- Mango Coconut Smoothie
- Island Style Fried Plantains
- Passion Fruit Cheesecake
- Tropical Chicken Salad
- Pineapple Upside-Down Cake
- Coconut Shrimp with Sweet Chili Sauce
- Barbados Style Flying Fish
- Caribbean Black Bean Soup
- Spicy Tamarind Shrimp Tacos
- Mango Chutney
- Pineapple Cilantro Salsa
- Plantain and Black Bean Empanadas
- Grilled Swordfish with Citrus Salsa
- Island Style Beef Kebabs
- Tropical Banana Bread
- Coconut Milk and Pineapple Popsicles

- Jamaican Beef Patties
- Sweet and Sour Mango Chicken
- Grilled Calamari with Lime Dressing
- Pineapple and Coconut Smoothie Bowl
- Caribbean Spiced Rice
- Passion Fruit Mojito
- Pineapple Basil Sorbet
- Plantain Chips with Avocado Dip
- Key Lime Curd Tarts
- Tropical Avocado and Mango Salad
- Coconut Macadamia Nut Cookies
- Caribbean Curried Chicken
- Grilled Banana with Rum Sauce
- Pineapple Coconut Muffins

Coconut Crusted Mahi Mahi

Ingredients:

- **4 mahi mahi fillets** (about 6 oz each)
- **1 cup shredded coconut** (unsweetened or sweetened, based on your preference)
- **1/2 cup panko breadcrumbs**
- **1/2 cup all-purpose flour**
- **2 large eggs**
- **1 tablespoon coconut oil** (or vegetable oil)
- **1 teaspoon garlic powder**
- **1 teaspoon onion powder**
- **1/2 teaspoon paprika**
- **1/2 teaspoon salt**
- **1/4 teaspoon black pepper**
- **Lemon wedges** (for serving)

Instructions:

1. **Preheat Oven and Prepare Baking Sheet:**
    - Preheat your oven to 400°F (200°C). Line a baking sheet with parchment paper or lightly grease it with cooking spray.
2. **Prepare Breading Stations:**
    - In one shallow dish, place the flour.
    - In a second shallow dish, beat the eggs.
    - In a third shallow dish, combine the shredded coconut, panko breadcrumbs, garlic powder, onion powder, paprika, salt, and black pepper.
3. **Coat the Mahi Mahi:**
    - Dredge each mahi mahi fillet in the flour, shaking off the excess.
    - Dip the floured fillet into the beaten eggs, allowing any excess to drip off.
    - Press the fillet into the coconut mixture, ensuring it is well coated with the coconut and breadcrumb mixture. Press down firmly to help the coating adhere.
4. **Cook the Mahi Mahi:**
    - Heat the coconut oil in a large skillet over medium-high heat. Once hot, add the coated mahi mahi fillets and cook for about 2-3 minutes per side, or until golden brown and crispy. You may need to do this in batches if your skillet isn't large enough.
    - Transfer the fillets to the prepared baking sheet and finish cooking in the preheated oven for an additional 5-7 minutes, or until the fish flakes easily with a fork and reaches an internal temperature of 145°F (63°C).
5. **Serve:**
    - Remove the mahi mahi from the oven and let it rest for a few minutes before serving.
    - Serve with lemon wedges for a fresh burst of citrus.

Tips:

- **Oil:** If you prefer, you can bake the fillets instead of pan-frying them. Brush them lightly with coconut oil and bake at 400°F (200°C) for 15-20 minutes, or until the coating is crispy and the fish is cooked through.
- **Coconut:** Adjust the amount of coconut and panko based on your preference for crunchiness and sweetness.
- **Side Dishes:** Coconut crusted mahi mahi pairs well with a variety of sides, such as a tropical fruit salsa, jasmine rice, or a fresh green salad.

This coconut crusted mahi mahi offers a delightful combination of crispy coconut and tender fish, perfect for a tropical-inspired meal. Enjoy this flavorful dish any time you want to bring a touch of the islands to your dining table!

Pineapple Teriyaki Chicken Skewers

Ingredients:

For the Marinade:

- **1/2 cup teriyaki sauce** (store-bought or homemade)
- **1/4 cup pineapple juice**
- **2 tablespoons honey** (or brown sugar)
- **2 tablespoons rice vinegar** (or apple cider vinegar)
- **2 cloves garlic, minced**
- **1 teaspoon fresh ginger, minced** (or 1/2 teaspoon ground ginger)

For the Skewers:

- **1 1/2 pounds boneless, skinless chicken breasts** (cut into 1-inch cubes)
- **1 cup fresh pineapple chunks** (about 1-inch pieces)
- **1 red bell pepper** (cut into 1-inch pieces)
- **1 green bell pepper** (cut into 1-inch pieces)
- **1 small red onion** (cut into 1-inch pieces)
- **Olive oil or cooking spray** (for grilling)

For Garnish (Optional):

- **Chopped fresh cilantro**
- **Sesame seeds**

Instructions:

1. **Prepare the Marinade:**
   - In a bowl, whisk together the teriyaki sauce, pineapple juice, honey, rice vinegar, minced garlic, and minced ginger until well combined.
2. **Marinate the Chicken:**
   - Place the chicken cubes in a large resealable plastic bag or bowl. Pour half of the marinade over the chicken and mix to coat evenly. Refrigerate for at least 30 minutes, or up to 4 hours for more flavor. Reserve the remaining marinade for basting.
3. **Prepare the Skewers:**
   - If using wooden skewers, soak them in water for at least 30 minutes to prevent burning. Thread the marinated chicken, pineapple chunks, bell peppers, and red onion onto the skewers, alternating between chicken and vegetables.
4. **Preheat Grill:**
   - Preheat your grill to medium-high heat. Lightly oil the grill grates or spray with cooking spray to prevent sticking.
5. **Grill the Skewers:**

- Place the skewers on the grill and cook for about 10-12 minutes, turning occasionally and basting with the reserved marinade, until the chicken is cooked through and has an internal temperature of 165°F (74°C). The vegetables should be tender and slightly charred.

6. **Serve:**
   - Remove the skewers from the grill and let them rest for a few minutes. Garnish with chopped fresh cilantro and sesame seeds, if desired.
7. **Enjoy:**
   - Serve the pineapple teriyaki chicken skewers with your favorite side dishes, such as steamed rice, a fresh salad, or grilled vegetables.

Tips:

- **Marinade:** For a deeper flavor, you can marinate the chicken overnight.
- **Grill:** If you don't have a grill, you can also cook these skewers on a grill pan or broil them in the oven.
- **Vegetables:** Feel free to add other vegetables to the skewers, such as zucchini, cherry tomatoes, or mushrooms.

These Pineapple Teriyaki Chicken Skewers are a delightful combination of sweet and savory flavors, perfect for a summer barbecue or a quick and tasty weeknight dinner. Enjoy the tropical taste and vibrant flavors of these delicious skewers!

Mango Salsa with Tortilla Chips

Ingredients:

- **2 ripe mangoes** (peeled, pitted, and diced)
- **1 small red onion** (finely chopped)
- **1 red bell pepper** (diced)
- **1 jalapeño pepper** (seeded and finely chopped; adjust for heat preference)
- **1/4 cup fresh cilantro** (chopped)
- **Juice of 1 lime**
- **1 tablespoon honey** (or agave syrup, optional for extra sweetness)
- **Salt and pepper** (to taste)

Instructions:

1. **Prepare the Ingredients:**
   - In a large bowl, combine the diced mangoes, chopped red onion, diced red bell pepper, and finely chopped jalapeño pepper.
2. **Add Cilantro and Lime Juice:**
   - Stir in the chopped cilantro and lime juice. If you prefer a slightly sweeter salsa, add the honey.
3. **Season:**
   - Season the salsa with salt and pepper to taste. Mix well to combine all the flavors.
4. **Chill:**
   - Cover and refrigerate the salsa for at least 30 minutes to allow the flavors to meld. Stir gently before serving.

Homemade Tortilla Chips

Ingredients:

- **6 small flour or corn tortillas**
- **2 tablespoons olive oil** (or vegetable oil)
- **1/2 teaspoon salt** (or to taste)
- **1/2 teaspoon ground cumin** (optional, for extra flavor)
- **1/2 teaspoon paprika** (optional, for extra color)

Instructions:

1. **Preheat Oven:**
   - Preheat your oven to 350°F (175°C). Line a baking sheet with parchment paper.
2. **Cut Tortillas:**
   - Stack the tortillas and cut them into wedges or triangles, about 6-8 pieces per tortilla.
3. **Season Tortillas:**
   - Brush the tortilla wedges lightly with olive oil and sprinkle with salt. If using, add ground cumin and paprika for extra flavor.
4. **Bake Chips:**
   - Arrange the tortilla wedges in a single layer on the prepared baking sheet. Bake for 8-10 minutes, or until they are crispy and lightly golden. Keep an eye on them to avoid burning.
5. **Cool:**
   - Allow the chips to cool completely on a wire rack. They will crisp up further as they cool.
6. **Serve:**
   - Serve the mango salsa with the homemade tortilla chips.

Tips:

- **Mango:** Use ripe but firm mangoes for the best texture in the salsa. Overripe mangoes may become mushy.
- **Heat:** Adjust the amount of jalapeño pepper based on your heat preference. For a milder salsa, use less or remove the seeds.
- **Storage:** Store leftover salsa in an airtight container in the refrigerator for up to 3 days. The tortilla chips can be kept in an airtight container at room temperature for up to a week.

This mango salsa with tortilla chips is a perfect combination of sweet, tangy, and crunchy flavors that everyone will enjoy. It's great for parties, picnics, or just a casual snack!

Island Style BBQ Ribs

Ingredients:

For the Ribs:

- **2 racks of baby back ribs** (about 2-3 pounds each)
- **Salt and pepper** (to taste)

For the Island BBQ Sauce:

- **1 cup pineapple juice**
- **1/2 cup ketchup**
- **1/4 cup soy sauce** (or tamari for gluten-free)
- **1/4 cup brown sugar**
- **2 tablespoons honey**
- **2 tablespoons apple cider vinegar**
- **2 tablespoons grated fresh ginger** (or 1 tablespoon ground ginger)
- **2 cloves garlic, minced**
- **1 tablespoon Dijon mustard**
- **1 teaspoon ground allspice**
- **1/2 teaspoon ground cumin**
- **1/2 teaspoon smoked paprika**
- **1/4 teaspoon cayenne pepper** (optional, for heat)

For Garnish:

- **Chopped fresh cilantro**
- **Sliced green onions**

Instructions:

1. **Prepare the Ribs:**
    - Preheat your oven to 300°F (150°C).
    - Remove the membrane from the back of the ribs (if not already removed). This can be done by loosening it with a knife and pulling it off.
    - Season both sides of the ribs with salt and pepper.
2. **Bake the Ribs:**
    - Place the ribs on a large piece of aluminum foil, bone side down. Wrap them tightly in the foil and place them on a baking sheet.
    - Bake in the preheated oven for 2.5 to 3 hours, or until the ribs are tender and cooked through.
3. **Prepare the BBQ Sauce:**
    - While the ribs are baking, combine pineapple juice, ketchup, soy sauce, brown sugar, honey, apple cider vinegar, grated ginger, minced garlic, Dijon mustard,

allspice, ground cumin, smoked paprika, and cayenne pepper in a medium saucepan.
     - Bring the mixture to a simmer over medium heat, stirring occasionally. Cook for about 10-15 minutes, or until the sauce has thickened slightly. Remove from heat and let cool.
4. **Grill the Ribs:**
     - Preheat your grill to medium-high heat.
     - Carefully remove the ribs from the foil and place them on the grill. Brush generously with the island BBQ sauce.
     - Grill the ribs for 5-7 minutes per side, basting with additional sauce and turning occasionally, until they are caramelized and have a nice char.
5. **Serve:**
     - Remove the ribs from the grill and let them rest for a few minutes before slicing.
     - Garnish with chopped fresh cilantro and sliced green onions, if desired.
6. **Enjoy:**
     - Serve the island style BBQ ribs with your favorite sides, such as coconut rice, grilled vegetables, or a fresh tropical salad.

Tips:

- **Tender Ribs:** Baking the ribs wrapped in foil ensures they are tender before grilling. The low and slow cooking process helps to break down the meat.
- **Sauce:** Feel free to adjust the sweetness or heat of the BBQ sauce according to your taste preferences. Add more honey or cayenne pepper as desired.
- **Grilling:** If you prefer, you can finish the ribs in the oven under the broiler instead of grilling, for a similar caramelized effect.

These Island Style BBQ Ribs are packed with tropical flavors and make a fantastic addition to any summer barbecue or casual meal. Enjoy the taste of the islands with every bite!

Caribbean Jerk Shrimp

Ingredients:

For the Jerk Marinade:

- **2 tablespoons allspice**
- **1 tablespoon dried thyme**
- **1 tablespoon smoked paprika**
- **1 teaspoon ground cinnamon**
- **1 teaspoon ground nutmeg**
- **1 teaspoon cayenne pepper** (adjust to taste for heat)
- **1 teaspoon garlic powder**
- **1 teaspoon onion powder**
- **1/2 teaspoon salt**
- **1/2 teaspoon black pepper**
- **1/2 teaspoon brown sugar** (optional, for a touch of sweetness)
- **2 tablespoons soy sauce** (or tamari for gluten-free)
- **2 tablespoons olive oil**
- **2 tablespoons lime juice**
- **2 cloves garlic, minced**
- **1 small piece of ginger** (about 1 inch, peeled and minced)

For the Shrimp:

- **1 pound large shrimp** (peeled and deveined)
- **1 tablespoon olive oil** (for cooking)

Instructions:

1. **Prepare the Jerk Marinade:**
   - In a bowl, combine all the jerk marinade ingredients: allspice, thyme, smoked paprika, cinnamon, nutmeg, cayenne pepper, garlic powder, onion powder, salt, black pepper, brown sugar (if using), soy sauce, olive oil, lime juice, minced garlic, and minced ginger. Mix well to combine.
2. **Marinate the Shrimp:**
   - Place the shrimp in a large bowl or resealable plastic bag. Pour the jerk marinade over the shrimp and toss to coat evenly.
   - Cover the bowl or seal the bag and refrigerate for at least 30 minutes, or up to 2 hours for more intense flavor.
3. **Cook the Shrimp:**
   - Heat a grill or a grill pan over medium-high heat. Brush the grill grates or pan with a little olive oil to prevent sticking.
   - Thread the marinated shrimp onto skewers (if using wooden skewers, soak them in water for 30 minutes beforehand).

- Grill the shrimp for about 2-3 minutes per side, or until they turn pink and opaque and are cooked through. Be careful not to overcook them.
4. **Serve:**
    - Remove the shrimp from the grill and let them rest for a minute or two.
    - Serve the Caribbean jerk shrimp with your favorite sides, such as coconut rice, a fresh tropical salad, or grilled vegetables.

Tips:

- **Marinade:** For best results, marinate the shrimp for at least 30 minutes, but if you have more time, marinating them overnight will deepen the flavors.
- **Heat Level:** Adjust the amount of cayenne pepper in the marinade based on your heat preference. You can also add a pinch of sugar if you prefer a slightly sweeter jerk flavor.
- **Cooking:** If you don't have a grill, you can also cook the shrimp in a skillet over medium-high heat or broil them in the oven.

Caribbean Jerk Shrimp is perfect for a summer barbecue or a quick and flavorful weeknight dinner. The spicy and aromatic jerk seasoning brings a taste of the Caribbean to your kitchen!

Ahi Tuna Poke Bowl

Ingredients:

For the Tuna Marinade:

- **1 pound ahi tuna** (sushi-grade, diced into 1/2-inch cubes)
- **1/4 cup soy sauce** (or tamari for gluten-free)
- **2 tablespoons sesame oil**
- **1 tablespoon rice vinegar**
- **1 tablespoon honey** (or agave syrup)
- **1 teaspoon freshly grated ginger**
- **1 clove garlic, minced**
- **1 teaspoon sesame seeds** (optional)

For the Bowl:

- **2 cups sushi rice** (or short-grain rice, cooked according to package instructions)
- **1 avocado** (sliced)
- **1/2 cucumber** (sliced into thin rounds)
- **1/2 cup edamame** (cooked and shelled)
- **1 small carrot** (julienned or shredded)
- **1/4 cup pickled ginger**
- **1/4 cup thinly sliced red cabbage**
- **1 tablespoon chopped fresh cilantro** (optional)
- **1 tablespoon sliced green onions**
- **Seaweed salad** (optional, for serving)
- **Sriracha or spicy mayo** (optional, for drizzling)

Instructions:

1. **Prepare the Tuna Marinade:**
   - In a medium bowl, whisk together the soy sauce, sesame oil, rice vinegar, honey, grated ginger, minced garlic, and sesame seeds.
   - Add the diced tuna to the marinade and gently toss to coat. Cover and refrigerate for at least 15 minutes, allowing the flavors to meld.
2. **Prepare the Rice:**
   - While the tuna is marinating, cook the sushi rice according to package instructions. Once cooked, let it cool slightly before serving.
3. **Assemble the Poke Bowl:**
   - Divide the cooked rice among serving bowls.
   - Arrange the marinated tuna on top of the rice.
   - Arrange the avocado slices, cucumber rounds, edamame, shredded carrot, pickled ginger, and red cabbage around the tuna in the bowl.
4. **Garnish and Serve:**

- Garnish with chopped fresh cilantro and sliced green onions.
- Add a side of seaweed salad if desired.
- Drizzle with sriracha or spicy mayo for an extra kick, if you like.
5. **Enjoy:**
    - Serve the Ahi Tuna Poke Bowl immediately for the freshest taste.

Tips:

- **Tuna:** Make sure to use sushi-grade tuna for the best flavor and safety. Freshness is key for a great poke bowl.
- **Marinade:** Adjust the sweetness or saltiness of the marinade to your taste. You can also add a splash of lime juice for extra tang.
- **Toppings:** Feel free to customize your poke bowl with your favorite toppings, such as radishes, cherry tomatoes, or pickled vegetables.

Ahi Tuna Poke Bowl is a delicious and healthy meal that's perfect for a quick lunch or dinner. The combination of fresh tuna, flavorful marinade, and colorful toppings makes for a satisfying and visually appealing dish. Enjoy your homemade poke bowl!

Tropical Fruit Salad

Ingredients:

- **1 pineapple** (peeled, cored, and cut into bite-sized pieces)
- **2 mangos** (peeled and diced)
- **2 kiwis** (peeled and sliced)
- **1 cup strawberries** (hulled and halved)
- **1 cup blueberries**
- **1 banana** (sliced)
- **1/2 cup shredded coconut** (optional, for garnish)
- **1/4 cup fresh mint leaves** (chopped, for garnish)

For the Dressing (Optional):

- **2 tablespoons honey** (or agave syrup)
- **1 tablespoon lime juice**
- **1 teaspoon grated fresh ginger** (optional, for extra zing)

Instructions:

1. **Prepare the Fruit:**
   - In a large bowl, combine the pineapple, mango, kiwi, strawberries, blueberries, and banana. Gently toss the fruit to mix.
2. **Make the Dressing (Optional):**
   - If using the dressing, whisk together the honey, lime juice, and grated ginger (if using) in a small bowl until well combined.
3. **Toss with Dressing:**
   - Drizzle the dressing over the fruit salad and gently toss to coat. Be careful not to mash the fruit.
4. **Garnish:**
   - Sprinkle shredded coconut and chopped fresh mint leaves over the top of the fruit salad.
5. **Serve:**
   - Serve immediately for the freshest taste. You can also refrigerate the salad for up to 2 hours before serving.

Tips:

- **Fruit:** Feel free to use other tropical fruits like papaya, passion fruit, or starfruit based on availability and preference.
- **Ripeness:** Ensure all fruit is ripe but firm to avoid mushiness.
- **Dressing:** The dressing is optional, but it adds a nice touch of sweetness and tang. Adjust the amount of honey or lime juice based on your taste preferences.

Tropical Fruit Salad is a delightful and healthy option that captures the essence of tropical flavors. Enjoy it as a refreshing snack or a sweet complement to any meal!

Jamaican Jerk Chicken

Ingredients:

For the Jerk Marinade:

- **2 tablespoons allspice**
- **1 tablespoon dried thyme**
- **1 tablespoon smoked paprika**
- **1 teaspoon ground cinnamon**
- **1 teaspoon ground nutmeg**
- **1 teaspoon cayenne pepper** (adjust to taste for heat)
- **1 teaspoon garlic powder**
- **1 teaspoon onion powder**
- **1/2 teaspoon salt**
- **1/2 teaspoon black pepper**
- **2 tablespoons brown sugar** (or honey)
- **1/4 cup soy sauce** (or tamari for gluten-free)
- **2 tablespoons vegetable oil** (or olive oil)
- **2 tablespoons lime juice**
- **2 cloves garlic, minced**
- **1 small piece of ginger** (about 1 inch, peeled and minced)
- **1-2 Scotch bonnet peppers** (seeded and chopped, adjust for heat; substitute with habanero peppers if needed)
- **1 small onion** (chopped)
- **1/2 cup green onions** (chopped)

For the Chicken:

- **4-6 bone-in, skinless chicken thighs** (or drumsticks)
- **1 tablespoon vegetable oil** (for grilling or roasting)

Instructions:

1. **Prepare the Marinade:**
   - In a food processor or blender, combine all the jerk marinade ingredients: allspice, thyme, smoked paprika, cinnamon, nutmeg, cayenne pepper, garlic powder, onion powder, salt, black pepper, brown sugar, soy sauce, vegetable oil, lime juice, minced garlic, minced ginger, Scotch bonnet peppers, onion, and green onions.
   - Blend until smooth. You may need to add a bit of water to achieve the right consistency.
2. **Marinate the Chicken:**
   - Place the chicken thighs in a large resealable plastic bag or bowl. Pour the jerk marinade over the chicken and toss to coat evenly.

- Seal the bag or cover the bowl and refrigerate for at least 2 hours, or preferably overnight, to allow the flavors to penetrate the meat.
3. **Preheat the Grill or Oven:**
    - If grilling, preheat your grill to medium-high heat. If roasting, preheat your oven to 375°F (190°C).
4. **Cook the Chicken:**
    - For grilling: Lightly oil the grill grates to prevent sticking. Grill the chicken for about 6-8 minutes per side, or until the internal temperature reaches 165°F (74°C) and the chicken is cooked through. Baste with additional marinade during grilling if desired.
    - For roasting: Place the marinated chicken on a baking sheet lined with parchment paper. Roast for 35-45 minutes, or until the chicken is cooked through and has an internal temperature of 165°F (74°C). You can broil for a few minutes at the end to get a crispy skin if desired.
5. **Serve:**
    - Remove the chicken from the grill or oven and let it rest for a few minutes before serving.
    - Serve the jerk chicken with your favorite sides, such as rice and peas, fried plantains, or a fresh salad.

Tips:

- **Heat Level:** Adjust the amount of Scotch bonnet peppers or cayenne pepper based on your heat tolerance. Scotch bonnet peppers are very spicy, so use them sparingly if you're sensitive to heat.
- **Marinade:** For the best flavor, marinate the chicken for as long as possible. Overnight marinating works best.
- **Grilling:** If you don't have a grill, you can also cook the chicken in a grill pan on the stovetop or broil it in the oven.

Jamaican Jerk Chicken is a flavorful and exciting dish that brings a taste of the Caribbean to your table. Enjoy the spicy, aromatic flavors and the delicious results of this classic recipe!

Pineapple Coconut Rice

Ingredients:

- **1 cup jasmine rice** (or basmati rice)
- **1 cup coconut milk** (full-fat for creaminess)
- **1 cup pineapple juice** (preferably unsweetened)
- **1/2 cup diced fresh pineapple** (or canned pineapple, drained)
- **1 tablespoon olive oil** (or coconut oil)
- **1/2 teaspoon salt**
- **1/4 teaspoon ground black pepper** (optional)
- **1/4 cup chopped fresh cilantro** (for garnish)
- **1 tablespoon toasted coconut flakes** (optional, for garnish)
- **Lime wedges** (for serving, optional)

Instructions:

1. **Rinse the Rice:**
   - Rinse the jasmine rice under cold water until the water runs clear. This helps to remove excess starch and prevent the rice from becoming sticky.
2. **Cook the Rice:**
   - In a medium saucepan, heat the olive oil (or coconut oil) over medium heat. Add the rinsed rice and cook for 1-2 minutes, stirring occasionally, until the rice is lightly toasted.
3. **Add Liquids:**
   - Pour in the coconut milk, pineapple juice, and salt. Stir to combine.
4. **Simmer:**
   - Bring the mixture to a boil over medium-high heat. Reduce the heat to low, cover the saucepan with a tight-fitting lid, and simmer for about 15-18 minutes, or until the rice is tender and the liquid has been absorbed.
5. **Add Pineapple:**
   - Once the rice is cooked, gently fold in the diced pineapple. Cover and let the rice sit for 5 minutes to allow the pineapple flavors to blend with the rice.
6. **Fluff and Garnish:**
   - Fluff the rice with a fork. Garnish with chopped fresh cilantro and toasted coconut flakes, if desired.
7. **Serve:**
   - Serve the Pineapple Coconut Rice warm, with lime wedges on the side if you like a touch of acidity.

Tips:

- **Rice:** Jasmine rice is preferred for its fragrant flavor and texture, but basmati rice can also be used if jasmine isn't available.

- **Pineapple:** Fresh pineapple adds a great texture, but canned pineapple works well too. Make sure to drain it thoroughly if using canned.
- **Coconut Milk:** For a richer flavor, use full-fat coconut milk. Light coconut milk can be used for a lower-calorie option.

Pineapple Coconut Rice is a delicious and exotic side dish that pairs wonderfully with grilled meats, seafood, or tropical-inspired dishes. Enjoy the sweet and creamy flavors of this easy-to-make recipe!

Spicy Papaya Salsa

Ingredients:

- **1 ripe papaya** (peeled, seeded, and diced)
- **1 red bell pepper** (diced)
- **1 small red onion** (finely diced)
- **1 jalapeño pepper** (seeded and finely chopped, adjust for heat)
- **1/4 cup fresh cilantro** (chopped)
- **1 lime** (juiced)
- **1 tablespoon honey** (or agave syrup)
- **1/2 teaspoon ground cumin**
- **Salt and black pepper** (to taste)

Instructions:

1. **Prepare the Papaya:**
    - Peel the papaya, cut it in half, and remove the seeds. Dice the flesh into small cubes and place in a large mixing bowl.
2. **Add Vegetables:**
    - Add the diced red bell pepper, finely diced red onion, and chopped jalapeño pepper to the bowl with the papaya.
3. **Mix in the Flavorings:**
    - Stir in the fresh cilantro, lime juice, honey, and ground cumin. Mix well to combine all the ingredients.
4. **Season:**
    - Taste the salsa and season with salt and black pepper as needed. Adjust the amount of jalapeño based on your heat preference.
5. **Chill:**
    - For best flavor, cover the salsa and refrigerate for at least 30 minutes to allow the flavors to meld.
6. **Serve:**
    - Serve the Spicy Papaya Salsa with grilled meats, seafood, or as a refreshing dip with tortilla chips.

Tips:

- **Heat Level:** Adjust the amount of jalapeño to control the spiciness. You can also remove the seeds and ribs of the jalapeño for less heat.
- **Papaya:** Make sure the papaya is ripe but firm for the best texture and sweetness. Overripe papaya can become mushy.
- **Variations:** Feel free to add other ingredients like diced mango, cucumber, or a splash of vinegar for added tang.

Spicy Papaya Salsa is a delightful and tropical twist on traditional salsa. Its sweet and spicy profile makes it a versatile addition to many dishes. Enjoy the fresh and zesty flavors!

Grilled Lobster with Garlic Butter

Ingredients:

For the Lobster:

- **4 lobster tails** (split in half lengthwise)
- **2 tablespoons olive oil**
- **1 teaspoon paprika**
- **1/2 teaspoon salt**
- **1/2 teaspoon black pepper**

For the Garlic Butter:

- **1/2 cup unsalted butter** (1 stick)
- **3 cloves garlic** (minced)
- **1 tablespoon fresh parsley** (chopped)
- **1 tablespoon lemon juice**
- **1/2 teaspoon dried thyme** (optional)
- **1/4 teaspoon red pepper flakes** (optional, for a bit of heat)

Instructions:

1. **Prepare the Lobster Tails:**
   - Use kitchen scissors to split each lobster tail lengthwise. If you prefer, you can use a knife to carefully cut through the shell, leaving the meat attached. This will allow the lobster meat to cook evenly and absorb the flavors of the garlic butter.
2. **Season the Lobster:**
   - Brush the lobster meat with olive oil and season with paprika, salt, and black pepper.
3. **Preheat the Grill:**
   - Preheat your grill to medium-high heat. If using a charcoal grill, ensure the coals are evenly distributed and at a consistent temperature.
4. **Grill the Lobster:**
   - Place the lobster tails shell-side down on the grill. Grill for about 5-7 minutes, or until the meat is opaque and cooked through. The exact cooking time may vary based on the size of the lobster tails. Flip the lobster tails halfway through cooking for even grill marks and flavor.
5. **Prepare the Garlic Butter:**
   - While the lobster is grilling, melt the butter in a small saucepan over medium heat. Add the minced garlic and cook for about 1-2 minutes, until fragrant but not browned.
   - Stir in the chopped parsley, lemon juice, dried thyme (if using), and red pepper flakes (if using). Remove from heat and keep warm.
6. **Baste with Garlic Butter:**

- During the last few minutes of grilling, brush the lobster meat with the garlic butter for added flavor.
7. **Serve:**
    - Remove the lobster from the grill and brush with more garlic butter.
    - Serve immediately with extra garlic butter on the side for dipping, and garnished with additional parsley if desired.

Tips:

- **Lobster:** Choose fresh or thawed lobster tails. If using frozen, ensure they are completely thawed before grilling.
- **Butter:** Be careful not to overcook the lobster as it can become tough. The meat should be firm and opaque.
- **Grill:** If the grill grates are too hot and you're worried about burning the lobster, use a piece of aluminum foil or a grill mat to prevent direct contact.

Grilled Lobster with Garlic Butter is an indulgent and impressive dish that highlights the natural sweetness of the lobster while adding a rich, buttery flavor. Enjoy this delicious treat at your next gathering or as a special dinner for yourself!

Key Lime Pie

Ingredients:

For the Graham Cracker Crust:

- **1 1/2 cups graham cracker crumbs** (about 10-12 whole graham crackers, crushed)
- **1/4 cup granulated sugar**
- **1/2 cup unsalted butter** (melted)

For the Key Lime Filling:

- **1 can (14 ounces) sweetened condensed milk**
- **1/2 cup sour cream**
- **1/2 cup fresh key lime juice** (about 6-8 key limes or use regular lime juice)
- **1 tablespoon lime zest** (optional, for added flavor)

For the Whipped Cream Topping:

- **1 cup heavy cream**
- **2 tablespoons powdered sugar**
- **1 teaspoon vanilla extract**

Instructions:

1. **Prepare the Graham Cracker Crust:**
    - Preheat your oven to 350°F (175°C).
    - In a medium bowl, combine the graham cracker crumbs, granulated sugar, and melted butter. Mix until the crumbs are evenly coated and the mixture resembles wet sand.
    - Press the crumb mixture firmly into the bottom and up the sides of a 9-inch pie pan to form an even crust.
    - Bake the crust in the preheated oven for 8-10 minutes, or until lightly golden and set. Allow it to cool completely before adding the filling.
2. **Make the Key Lime Filling:**
    - In a large bowl, whisk together the sweetened condensed milk, sour cream, and key lime juice until smooth and well combined. If using, mix in the lime zest for additional flavor.
    - Pour the filling into the cooled graham cracker crust and spread it evenly.
3. **Bake the Pie:**
    - Bake the pie in the preheated oven for 10-12 minutes, or until the filling is set and slightly jiggly in the center.
    - Turn off the oven and leave the pie in the oven with the door slightly ajar for about 1 hour to cool gradually.
4. **Chill the Pie:**

- After the pie has cooled, cover it with plastic wrap and refrigerate for at least 4 hours, or overnight, to fully set and chill.
5. **Prepare the Whipped Cream Topping:**
    - In a chilled mixing bowl, beat the heavy cream with an electric mixer on medium-high speed until soft peaks form.
    - Add the powdered sugar and vanilla extract, and continue to beat until stiff peaks form.
6. **Serve:**
    - Spread or pipe the whipped cream over the chilled pie.
    - Garnish with additional lime zest or thin lime slices, if desired.

Tips:

- **Key Limes:** Key limes have a distinct tartness compared to regular limes. If you can't find key limes, regular lime juice works fine, but the flavor will be slightly different.
- **Crust:** For an extra-crispy crust, you can chill it in the refrigerator for about 30 minutes before baking.
- **Setting:** The pie needs to chill thoroughly to set properly. Don't rush this step for the best texture.

Key Lime Pie is a delightful dessert with a perfect balance of tart and sweet flavors, complemented by a rich graham cracker crust. Enjoy this classic treat at your next gathering or as a refreshing end to any meal!

Coconut Curry Fish Stew

Ingredients:

For the Stew:

- **1 lb (450g) firm white fish fillets** (such as cod, tilapia, or snapper), cut into bite-sized pieces
- **1 tablespoon vegetable oil**
- **1 onion**, finely chopped
- **3 cloves garlic**, minced
- **1 tablespoon fresh ginger**, minced
- **1 red bell pepper**, diced
- **1 medium carrot**, sliced
- **1 zucchini**, sliced
- **1 can (14 ounces) coconut milk** (full-fat for creaminess)
- **1 cup fish or vegetable broth**
- **2 tablespoons red curry paste** (adjust to taste)
- **1 tablespoon fish sauce** (or soy sauce for a vegetarian option)
- **1 tablespoon brown sugar** (or honey)
- **1 tablespoon lime juice** (freshly squeezed)
- **1 cup cherry tomatoes**, halved
- **2 cups baby spinach** (or regular spinach)
- **Fresh cilantro**, chopped (for garnish)

For Serving:

- **Steamed jasmine rice** or **basmati rice**

Instructions:

1. **Prepare the Fish:**
    - Cut the fish into bite-sized pieces and set aside.
2. **Cook the Aromatics:**
    - Heat the vegetable oil in a large pot or Dutch oven over medium heat.
    - Add the chopped onion and cook for 3-4 minutes, until softened.
    - Stir in the minced garlic and ginger, and cook for an additional 1-2 minutes until fragrant.
3. **Add Vegetables:**
    - Add the diced red bell pepper, sliced carrot, and zucchini to the pot. Cook for about 5 minutes, stirring occasionally, until the vegetables start to soften.
4. **Add Curry Paste and Liquids:**
    - Stir in the red curry paste and cook for 1 minute to release its flavors.
    - Pour in the coconut milk and fish or vegetable broth. Stir well to combine.

- Add the fish sauce (or soy sauce), brown sugar, and lime juice. Bring the mixture to a gentle simmer.

5. **Simmer the Stew:**
   - Reduce the heat to low and let the stew simmer for 10 minutes, allowing the flavors to meld and the vegetables to become tender.
6. **Add Fish and Tomatoes:**
   - Gently add the fish pieces and cherry tomatoes to the stew. Cook for an additional 5-7 minutes, or until the fish is cooked through and opaque. Be careful not to overcook the fish.
7. **Add Spinach:**
   - Stir in the baby spinach and cook for 1-2 minutes until wilted.
8. **Adjust Seasonings:**
   - Taste the stew and adjust the seasoning with additional salt, pepper, or lime juice as needed.
9. **Serve:**
   - Ladle the stew over steamed jasmine or basmati rice.
   - Garnish with chopped fresh cilantro.

Tips:

- **Fish:** Choose a firm white fish that will hold its shape during cooking. Avoid very delicate fish as it may break apart.
- **Curry Paste:** Adjust the amount of red curry paste based on your preference for spiciness. Start with less and add more if needed.
- **Vegetables:** Feel free to use other vegetables like bell peppers or sweet potatoes based on your preference.

Coconut Curry Fish Stew is a delightful dish that combines the creaminess of coconut milk with the bold flavors of curry. It's both comforting and exotic, making it a great choice for a satisfying meal. Enjoy this flavorful stew with your favorite rice for a complete and delicious dinner!

Rum Punch

Ingredients:

- **1 cup light rum**
- **1/2 cup dark rum**
- **1 cup pineapple juice**
- **1 cup orange juice**
- **1/4 cup lime juice** (freshly squeezed)
- **1/4 cup grenadine syrup** (for sweetness and color)
- **1/4 cup simple syrup** (adjust to taste, optional)
- **1/2 teaspoon Angostura bitters** (optional, for added depth)
- **Ice cubes**
- **Lime slices** (for garnish)
- **Orange slices** (for garnish)
- **Pineapple chunks** (for garnish)
- **Maraschino cherries** (for garnish)

Instructions:

1. **Mix the Punch:**
   - In a large pitcher or punch bowl, combine the light rum, dark rum, pineapple juice, orange juice, lime juice, and grenadine syrup.
   - If using, add the simple syrup and Angostura bitters. Stir well to combine all the ingredients.
2. **Chill:**
   - Refrigerate the punch for at least 1-2 hours to allow the flavors to meld and the punch to chill.
3. **Serve:**
   - Fill glasses or punch cups with ice cubes.
   - Pour the chilled punch over the ice.
4. **Garnish:**
   - Garnish each glass with lime slices, orange slices, pineapple chunks, and maraschino cherries.
5. **Optional:**
   - For a sparkling touch, top each glass with a splash of club soda or ginger ale just before serving.

Tips:

- **Rum:** You can adjust the ratio of light to dark rum based on your preference. Light rum provides a lighter flavor, while dark rum adds richness.
- **Sweetness:** Adjust the sweetness by adding more or less grenadine syrup and simple syrup according to your taste.

- **Fruit Juice:** Use fresh juices for the best flavor. Store-bought juices are convenient but might be less vibrant.
- **Bitters:** Angostura bitters add complexity but are optional if you prefer a simpler taste.

Rum Punch is versatile and can be customized with different fruit juices or additional spices, such as a cinnamon stick or a dash of nutmeg, for a unique twist. Enjoy this tropical treat at your next party or get-together!

Pineapple Ginger Glazed Ham

Ingredients:

For the Ham:

- **1 fully cooked bone-in ham** (about 8-10 pounds)
- **Whole cloves** (optional, for studding the ham)

For the Pineapple Ginger Glaze:

- **1 cup pineapple juice**
- **1/2 cup brown sugar**
- **1/4 cup honey**
- **2 tablespoons fresh ginger** (grated)
- **1/4 cup Dijon mustard**
- **2 tablespoons soy sauce**
- **1 tablespoon cornstarch** (optional, for thickening)
- **2 tablespoons water** (optional, for cornstarch slurry)

Instructions:

1. **Preheat the Oven:**
    - Preheat your oven to 325°F (165°C).
2. **Prepare the Ham:**
    - If the ham is not pre-sliced, score the surface of the ham in a diamond pattern with a sharp knife. This will help the glaze penetrate the meat.
    - Optionally, stud the ham with whole cloves by inserting them into the intersections of the scored lines.
3. **Prepare the Glaze:**
    - In a medium saucepan, combine the pineapple juice, brown sugar, honey, grated ginger, Dijon mustard, and soy sauce.
    - Bring the mixture to a simmer over medium heat, stirring occasionally until the sugar is dissolved and the ingredients are well combined.
4. **Thicken the Glaze (Optional):**
    - If you prefer a thicker glaze, mix the cornstarch and water in a small bowl to create a slurry.
    - Stir the slurry into the simmering glaze and cook for an additional 2-3 minutes, or until the glaze has thickened.
5. **Glaze the Ham:**
    - Place the ham in a roasting pan and brush it generously with the pineapple ginger glaze.
    - Cover the ham loosely with aluminum foil.
6. **Bake the Ham:**

- Bake the ham in the preheated oven for about 15-18 minutes per pound, or until heated through. Baste the ham with additional glaze every 20-30 minutes.
- During the last 30 minutes of baking, remove the foil and brush the ham with the glaze for a caramelized finish.

7. **Rest and Serve:**
   - Once the ham is heated through and caramelized, remove it from the oven and let it rest for about 15 minutes before slicing.
   - Serve with additional glaze on the side.

Tips:

- **Ham:** Use a fully cooked ham to simplify preparation. Bone-in hams are traditional and flavorful, but boneless or spiral-cut hams can also work.
- **Glaze:** Adjust the amount of ginger and honey based on your taste preferences. For extra spice, add a pinch of ground cloves or cinnamon to the glaze.
- **Serving:** Serve the ham with additional pineapple ginger glaze, along with your favorite sides.

Pineapple Ginger Glazed Ham is a flavorful and visually stunning dish that adds a touch of tropical sweetness and spice to your holiday table or any special occasion. Enjoy the delicious combination of flavors with family and friends!

Coconut Lime Chicken

Ingredients:

For the Marinade:

- **1/2 cup coconut milk** (full-fat for creaminess)
- **1/4 cup lime juice** (freshly squeezed)
- **2 tablespoons soy sauce** (or tamari for gluten-free)
- **2 tablespoons honey** (or maple syrup for a different sweetness)
- **3 cloves garlic** (minced)
- **1 tablespoon fresh ginger** (grated)
- **1 teaspoon ground cumin**
- **1/2 teaspoon paprika**
- **1/4 teaspoon ground coriander**
- **Salt and black pepper** (to taste)

For the Chicken:

- **4 boneless, skinless chicken breasts** (or thighs if preferred)
- **1 tablespoon vegetable oil** (for cooking)

For Garnish (Optional):

- **Chopped fresh cilantro**
- **Lime wedges**
- **Toasted coconut flakes**

Instructions:

1. **Prepare the Marinade:**
   - In a bowl, whisk together the coconut milk, lime juice, soy sauce, honey, minced garlic, grated ginger, ground cumin, paprika, ground coriander, salt, and black pepper.
2. **Marinate the Chicken:**
   - Place the chicken breasts in a large resealable plastic bag or shallow dish.
   - Pour the marinade over the chicken, making sure it is well coated.
   - Seal the bag or cover the dish and refrigerate for at least 1 hour, or up to 4 hours for more intense flavor.
3. **Cook the Chicken:**
   - Heat the vegetable oil in a large skillet over medium heat.
   - Remove the chicken from the marinade and let any excess drip off.
   - Cook the chicken in the skillet for 6-8 minutes per side, or until the chicken is cooked through and has an internal temperature of 165°F (74°C). Baste with any remaining marinade during cooking if desired.
4. **Serve:**

- Transfer the cooked chicken to a serving platter.
- Garnish with chopped fresh cilantro, lime wedges, and toasted coconut flakes if desired.

5. **Optional:**
    - For a richer sauce, you can simmer the remaining marinade in the skillet until it thickens slightly and drizzle it over the chicken.

Tips:

- **Chicken:** If you prefer, you can also use chicken thighs for a more flavorful and juicy option. Adjust the cooking time as needed.
- **Marinating Time:** Don't marinate the chicken for too long (beyond 4 hours) as the acidity from the lime juice can start to break down the meat too much.
- **Serving Suggestions:** Serve with steamed jasmine rice, quinoa, or a fresh salad for a complete meal. Coconut lime chicken pairs well with simple sides that complement its flavors.

Coconut Lime Chicken offers a delightful balance of creamy coconut and zesty lime, creating a deliciously tropical meal that's sure to impress. Enjoy the vibrant flavors and tender chicken with your favorite sides!

Bahamian Conch Fritters

Ingredients:

For the Fritters:

- **1 lb (450g) conch meat**, finely chopped (you can find it fresh or frozen at seafood markets)
- **1 cup all-purpose flour**
- **1/2 cup cornmeal**
- **1 teaspoon baking powder**
- **1/2 teaspoon salt**
- **1/2 teaspoon black pepper**
- **1/2 teaspoon paprika**
- **1/4 teaspoon cayenne pepper** (optional, for heat)
- **1/2 cup milk** (or coconut milk for a richer flavor)
- **2 large eggs**
- **1 small onion**, finely chopped
- **1 bell pepper** (red or green), finely chopped
- **2 cloves garlic**, minced
- **2 tablespoons fresh parsley**, chopped
- **1 tablespoon lime juice** (freshly squeezed)
- **1/4 cup scallions**, finely chopped
- **Vegetable oil** (for frying)

For the Dipping Sauce (optional):

- **1/2 cup mayonnaise**
- **2 tablespoons ketchup**
- **1 tablespoon lime juice**
- **1 teaspoon hot sauce** (or to taste)
- **1 teaspoon honey** (optional, for a touch of sweetness)

Instructions:

1. **Prepare the Conch:**
   - If using frozen conch, thaw it completely and drain well. Finely chop the conch meat and set aside.
2. **Make the Batter:**
   - In a large bowl, whisk together the flour, cornmeal, baking powder, salt, black pepper, paprika, and cayenne pepper.
   - In another bowl, combine the milk, eggs, and lime juice. Mix well.
   - Pour the wet ingredients into the dry ingredients and stir until just combined.
   - Fold in the chopped conch, onion, bell pepper, garlic, parsley, and scallions until evenly mixed.

3. **Heat the Oil:**
   - Heat about 2 inches of vegetable oil in a deep skillet or pot over medium-high heat. The oil should reach 350°F (175°C) for frying.
4. **Fry the Fritters:**
   - Drop spoonfuls of the fritter batter into the hot oil, being careful not to overcrowd the pan. Fry in batches if necessary.
   - Cook the fritters for 2-3 minutes on each side, or until golden brown and crispy. Use a slotted spoon to remove them from the oil and drain on paper towels.
5. **Prepare the Dipping Sauce (Optional):**
   - In a small bowl, mix together the mayonnaise, ketchup, lime juice, hot sauce, and honey (if using). Adjust the seasoning to taste.
6. **Serve:**
   - Serve the conch fritters hot, with the dipping sauce on the side if desired.

Tips:

- **Conch Meat:** Fresh conch is ideal, but frozen conch works well too. Ensure it is well-drained and chopped finely for the best texture.
- **Oil Temperature:** Maintain the oil temperature to ensure the fritters cook evenly and become crispy without absorbing too much oil.
- **Flavor Variations:** Feel free to experiment with additional spices or herbs to tailor the fritters to your taste.

Bahamian Conch Fritters are a delightful Caribbean treat with a crispy exterior and a flavorful, tender interior. Enjoy these fritters as a tasty appetizer or a savory snack, perfect for sharing with friends and family!

Grilled Pineapple with Cinnamon Sugar

Ingredients:

- **1 ripe pineapple**
- **2 tablespoons granulated sugar**
- **1 teaspoon ground cinnamon**
- **1 tablespoon butter** (melted, for brushing)
- **Optional: Fresh mint leaves** (for garnish)

Instructions:

1. **Prepare the Pineapple:**
    - Peel the pineapple and remove the core. Cut the pineapple into rings or wedges, about 1/2-inch thick. If you prefer, you can also cut the pineapple into spears.
2. **Make the Cinnamon Sugar:**
    - In a small bowl, combine the granulated sugar and ground cinnamon. Mix well and set aside.
3. **Preheat the Grill:**
    - Preheat your grill to medium-high heat. If using a stovetop grill pan, preheat it over medium-high heat as well.
4. **Prepare the Pineapple for Grilling:**
    - Brush the pineapple slices lightly with melted butter. This will help the cinnamon sugar adhere and add a nice caramelized flavor.
5. **Grill the Pineapple:**
    - Place the pineapple slices on the hot grill or grill pan. Grill for about 2-3 minutes per side, or until grill marks appear and the pineapple is slightly caramelized and softened. Avoid overcooking to keep the pineapple juicy.
6. **Add Cinnamon Sugar:**
    - Once the pineapple is grilled, sprinkle the cinnamon sugar mixture evenly over the hot pineapple slices.
7. **Serve:**
    - Serve the grilled pineapple warm. Garnish with fresh mint leaves if desired for a refreshing touch.

Tips:

- **Ripeness:** Choose a ripe pineapple for the best flavor. It should be fragrant and have a slight give when pressed.
- **Grilling:** Ensure your grill or grill pan is preheated to get a good sear and caramelization on the pineapple.
- **Serving Suggestions:** Grilled pineapple pairs wonderfully with vanilla ice cream, yogurt, or as a topping for desserts. You can also serve it as a side dish or alongside grilled meats.

Grilled Pineapple with Cinnamon Sugar is a simple yet elegant dessert that highlights the tropical sweetness of pineapple with a hint of spice. It's perfect for summer barbecues or any time you want a light and flavorful treat!

Guava BBQ Sauce

Ingredients:

- **1 cup guava paste** (or guava jelly, melted)
- **1/2 cup ketchup**
- **1/4 cup apple cider vinegar**
- **1/4 cup soy sauce**
- **1/4 cup brown sugar**
- **2 tablespoons Worcestershire sauce**
- **2 tablespoons Dijon mustard**
- **1 tablespoon fresh lime juice** (or lemon juice)
- **2 cloves garlic**, minced
- **1 teaspoon ground cumin**
- **1 teaspoon smoked paprika**
- **1/2 teaspoon ground black pepper**
- **1/2 teaspoon salt** (adjust to taste)
- **1/4 teaspoon cayenne pepper** (optional, for heat)

Instructions:

1. **Prepare Guava Paste:**
   - If using guava paste, cut it into small pieces and melt it slightly in the microwave or on the stovetop to make it easier to incorporate into the sauce. If using guava jelly, you can use it directly.
2. **Combine Ingredients:**
   - In a medium saucepan, combine the melted guava paste (or guava jelly), ketchup, apple cider vinegar, soy sauce, brown sugar, Worcestershire sauce, Dijon mustard, and lime juice.
3. **Add Spices:**
   - Stir in the minced garlic, ground cumin, smoked paprika, black pepper, salt, and cayenne pepper (if using).
4. **Simmer the Sauce:**
   - Place the saucepan over medium heat and bring the mixture to a simmer. Stir frequently to prevent burning and to ensure the sugar and guava paste dissolve completely.
5. **Cook:**
   - Reduce the heat to low and let the sauce simmer for about 10-15 minutes, or until it has thickened to your desired consistency. Stir occasionally.
6. **Adjust Seasonings:**
   - Taste the sauce and adjust the seasoning if necessary. You can add more salt, sugar, or lime juice to balance the flavors according to your preference.
7. **Cool and Store:**
   - Let the sauce cool to room temperature before using it. Store any leftover sauce in an airtight container in the refrigerator for up to 2 weeks.

Tips:

- **Guava Paste:** If you can't find guava paste, guava jelly or puree can be used as alternatives. Guava paste is often found in Latin American or specialty grocery stores.
- **Texture:** If you prefer a smoother sauce, you can blend it with an immersion blender or regular blender after cooking.
- **Heat Level:** Adjust the cayenne pepper to control the spiciness of the sauce. Omit it if you prefer a milder flavor.

Guava BBQ Sauce offers a tropical twist on traditional barbecue flavors, adding a sweet and fruity dimension that complements grilled meats beautifully. Enjoy this unique sauce at your next BBQ or cookout!

Caribbean Spiced Pork Tenderloin

Ingredients:

For the Spice Rub:

- **2 tablespoons ground allspice**
- **1 tablespoon ground cumin**
- **1 tablespoon paprika**
- **1 teaspoon ground cinnamon**
- **1 teaspoon garlic powder**
- **1 teaspoon onion powder**
- **1/2 teaspoon ground nutmeg**
- **1/2 teaspoon dried thyme**
- **1/2 teaspoon cayenne pepper** (optional, for heat)
- **Salt and black pepper** (to taste)

For the Pork:

- **2 pork tenderloins** (about 1 pound each)
- **2 tablespoons olive oil**
- **1 tablespoon fresh lime juice** (or lemon juice)
- **2 cloves garlic**, minced

For Garnish (Optional):

- **Fresh cilantro** (chopped)
- **Lime wedges**

Instructions:

1. **Prepare the Spice Rub:**
   - In a small bowl, combine the ground allspice, ground cumin, paprika, ground cinnamon, garlic powder, onion powder, ground nutmeg, dried thyme, cayenne pepper (if using), salt, and black pepper. Mix well.
2. **Season the Pork:**
   - Pat the pork tenderloins dry with paper towels. This helps the spice rub adhere better.
   - Rub the pork tenderloins all over with olive oil.
   - Sprinkle the spice mixture evenly over the pork, pressing it in with your hands to ensure it sticks.
3. **Marinate:**
   - Place the seasoned pork tenderloins in a resealable plastic bag or shallow dish.
   - Add the minced garlic and fresh lime juice, and toss to coat. Marinate in the refrigerator for at least 1 hour, or up to 4 hours for more intense flavor.
4. **Preheat the Oven:**

- Preheat your oven to 400°F (200°C).

5. **Sear the Pork:**
   - Heat a large oven-safe skillet over medium-high heat. Add a little olive oil if needed.
   - Once the skillet is hot, sear the pork tenderloins for 2-3 minutes per side, or until browned. This step adds flavor and helps lock in juices.

6. **Roast the Pork:**
   - Transfer the skillet to the preheated oven.
   - Roast the pork tenderloins for 20-25 minutes, or until the internal temperature reaches 145°F (63°C) when measured with a meat thermometer.

7. **Rest and Slice:**
   - Remove the pork from the oven and let it rest for about 5-10 minutes before slicing. This helps the juices redistribute and keeps the meat moist.

8. **Serve:**
   - Slice the pork tenderloin into medallions.
   - Garnish with chopped fresh cilantro and lime wedges if desired.

Tips:

- **Spice Rub:** Adjust the amount of cayenne pepper based on your heat preference. The rub can be made in advance and stored in an airtight container.
- **Searing:** Searing the pork before roasting helps develop a rich flavor and adds a nice crust. If you don't have an oven-safe skillet, you can sear the pork in a regular skillet and then transfer it to a baking dish for roasting.
- **Serving Suggestions:** Serve the pork tenderloin with Caribbean-style sides such as coconut rice, plantains, or a fresh mango salsa.

Caribbean Spiced Pork Tenderloin offers a vibrant and flavorful meal that brings a taste of the tropics to your table. Enjoy the aromatic spices and juicy pork with your favorite sides for a delicious dining experience!

Mango Coconut Smoothie

Ingredients:

- **1 cup fresh or frozen mango chunks**
- **1/2 cup coconut milk** (full-fat or light, depending on your preference)
- **1/2 cup Greek yogurt** (plain or vanilla, for added creaminess and protein)
- **1/2 cup orange juice** (or pineapple juice for a sweeter flavor)
- **1 tablespoon honey** (or maple syrup, to taste; adjust based on the sweetness of the mango)
- **1/2 teaspoon vanilla extract** (optional, for extra flavor)
- **1/2 cup ice** (if using fresh mango, or if you prefer a thicker, colder smoothie)

Instructions:

1. **Prepare Ingredients:**
   - If using fresh mango, peel and cut it into chunks. If using frozen mango, no need to thaw it.
   - Measure out the coconut milk, Greek yogurt, orange juice, and honey.
2. **Blend:**
   - Add the mango chunks, coconut milk, Greek yogurt, orange juice, honey, and vanilla extract (if using) to a blender.
   - Blend until smooth and creamy. If the smoothie is too thick, you can add a little more coconut milk or orange juice to reach your desired consistency.
3. **Add Ice (Optional):**
   - If you're using fresh mango and want a colder, thicker smoothie, add the ice to the blender and blend again until the ice is fully incorporated and the smoothie is frothy.
4. **Taste and Adjust:**
   - Taste the smoothie and adjust the sweetness if needed by adding a bit more honey or maple syrup.
5. **Serve:**
   - Pour the smoothie into glasses. You can garnish with a small piece of mango or a sprinkle of shredded coconut if desired.
6. **Enjoy:**
   - Serve immediately and enjoy the refreshing tropical flavors!

Tips:

- **Mango:** For the best flavor, use ripe mango. If you can't find fresh mango, frozen mango chunks are a convenient alternative.
- **Coconut Milk:** Full-fat coconut milk will give the smoothie a richer, creamier texture, while light coconut milk will make it a bit lighter.
- **Greek Yogurt:** For a dairy-free option, use coconut yogurt or another plant-based yogurt.

- **Blending:** If your blender struggles with frozen mango, let it sit out for a few minutes to soften slightly before blending.

A Mango Coconut Smoothie is not only delicious but also packed with vitamins and nutrients from the mango and coconut. It's a perfect way to cool down on a hot day or enjoy a taste of the tropics any time!

Island Style Fried Plantains

Ingredients:

- **2-3 ripe plantains** (yellow with black spots for sweetness, or green if you prefer a less sweet, more savory flavor)
- **Vegetable oil** (for frying)
- **Salt** (to taste)
- **Optional: Cinnamon sugar** (for a sweet version), **garlic powder** (for a savory twist)

Instructions:

1. **Prepare the Plantains:**
   - Peel the plantains. To do this, cut off the ends and make a lengthwise slit along the skin. Gently peel away the skin. For ripe plantains, the skin will come off easily. For green plantains, it may be a bit tougher.
   - Slice the plantains into rounds about 1/4-inch thick. For a different texture, you can slice them diagonally or into thin strips.
2. **Heat the Oil:**
   - Pour enough vegetable oil into a large skillet to cover the bottom by about 1/4 inch. Heat the oil over medium-high heat until it reaches 350°F (175°C). If you don't have a thermometer, you can test the oil by dropping in a small piece of plantain; it should sizzle and rise to the surface.
3. **Fry the Plantains:**
   - Carefully add the plantain slices to the hot oil in batches, making sure not to overcrowd the pan. Fry for about 2-3 minutes per side, or until the plantains are golden brown and crispy.
   - Use a slotted spoon to transfer the fried plantains to a plate lined with paper towels to drain any excess oil.
4. **Season the Plantains:**
   - While the plantains are still hot, sprinkle them with a pinch of salt. For a sweet variation, you can also sprinkle them with cinnamon sugar.
   - For a savory twist, consider adding a light dusting of garlic powder or a pinch of paprika.
5. **Serve:**
   - Serve the fried plantains warm as a snack, appetizer, or side dish. They pair well with a variety of dishes, from grilled meats to salads, or simply enjoy them on their own.

Tips:

- **Ripeness:** The sweetness of the plantains increases as they ripen. Use ripe plantains for a sweeter flavor, or green plantains for a more neutral, starchy taste.

- **Oil Temperature:** Maintaining the correct oil temperature is crucial for achieving crispy plantains without them absorbing too much oil. If the oil is too hot, the plantains may burn; if it's too cool, they may become greasy.
- **Serving Suggestions:** Fried plantains are delicious on their own but can also be served with dipping sauces such as a tangy aioli or a spicy salsa.

Island Style Fried Plantains are a versatile and delightful treat that brings a touch of the Caribbean to your table. Enjoy their sweet and crispy goodness as a snack, side dish, or party appetizer!

Passion Fruit Cheesecake

Ingredients:

For the Crust:

- **1 1/2 cups graham cracker crumbs** (about 12 whole graham crackers, crushed)
- **1/4 cup granulated sugar**
- **1/2 cup unsalted butter** (melted)

For the Cheesecake Filling:

- **4 (8-ounce) packages cream cheese** (softened)
- **1 cup granulated sugar**
- **1 teaspoon vanilla extract**
- **4 large eggs**
- **1 cup sour cream**
- **1 cup heavy cream**
- **1 cup passion fruit pulp** (fresh or store-bought, strained to remove seeds)

For the Passion Fruit Topping:

- **1/2 cup passion fruit pulp** (fresh or store-bought)
- **1/4 cup granulated sugar**
- **1 tablespoon cornstarch**
- **2 tablespoons water**

Instructions:

1. **Preheat the Oven:**
    - Preheat your oven to 325°F (163°C).
2. **Prepare the Crust:**
    - In a medium bowl, combine the graham cracker crumbs, granulated sugar, and melted butter. Mix until the crumbs are evenly coated and the mixture resembles wet sand.
    - Press the crumb mixture evenly into the bottom of a 9-inch springform pan. Use the back of a spoon or the bottom of a glass to press it down firmly.
    - Bake the crust for 10 minutes, then remove it from the oven and let it cool while you prepare the filling.
3. **Prepare the Cheesecake Filling:**
    - In a large mixing bowl, beat the softened cream cheese with an electric mixer on medium speed until smooth and creamy.
    - Gradually add the granulated sugar and beat until combined.
    - Add the vanilla extract and mix well.
    - Add the eggs one at a time, beating well after each addition. Scrape down the sides of the bowl as needed.

- Add the sour cream and heavy cream, and mix until smooth.
- Gently fold in the passion fruit pulp until evenly distributed.

4. **Bake the Cheesecake:**
   - Pour the cheesecake filling over the prepared crust in the springform pan.
   - Smooth the top with a spatula.
   - Place the pan on a baking sheet (to catch any drips) and bake for 60-70 minutes, or until the center is set but still slightly wobbly. The edges should be firm and the center should not jiggle excessively.
   - Turn off the oven and crack the oven door slightly. Let the cheesecake cool in the oven for about 1 hour. This helps prevent cracking.

5. **Chill the Cheesecake:**
   - After cooling, refrigerate the cheesecake for at least 4 hours, or overnight for best results. This allows the flavors to meld and the cheesecake to set properly.

6. **Prepare the Passion Fruit Topping:**
   - In a small saucepan, combine the passion fruit pulp, granulated sugar, cornstarch, and water.
   - Cook over medium heat, stirring constantly, until the mixture thickens and becomes clear (about 5-7 minutes).
   - Remove from heat and let it cool to room temperature.

7. **Top and Serve:**
   - Once the cheesecake is fully chilled, remove it from the springform pan.
   - Spread or drizzle the passion fruit topping evenly over the top of the cheesecake.
   - Garnish with additional passion fruit pulp or fresh fruit if desired.

8. **Enjoy:**
   - Slice the cheesecake and serve chilled. Enjoy the creamy, tropical flavors!

Tips:

- **Passion Fruit Pulp:** If fresh passion fruit is not available, use store-bought passion fruit pulp. Make sure to strain it to remove seeds if necessary.
- **Prevent Cracking:** To prevent cracking, avoid overmixing the batter and bake the cheesecake in a water bath if desired (wrap the pan in aluminum foil and place it in a larger pan with hot water).
- **Garnish:** For added flair, garnish the cheesecake with fresh fruit, mint leaves, or a sprinkle of lime zest.

Passion Fruit Cheesecake is a tropical delight that pairs the creamy texture of cheesecake with the bright, tangy flavor of passion fruit. It's a perfect way to end a meal on a sweet, exotic no

Tropical Chicken Salad

Ingredients:

- **2 cups cooked chicken breast** (diced or shredded)
- **1 cup fresh pineapple chunks** (or canned, drained)
- **1 cup mango chunks** (fresh or frozen, thawed)
- **1/2 cup red bell pepper** (diced)
- **1/2 cup red onion** (finely chopped)
- **1/4 cup fresh cilantro** (chopped)
- **1/4 cup chopped cashews** (or almonds)
- **1/4 cup shredded coconut** (toasted, optional)

For the Dressing:

- **1/2 cup plain Greek yogurt**
- **1/4 cup mayonnaise**
- **2 tablespoons lime juice**
- **1 tablespoon honey**
- **1 teaspoon ground cumin**
- **Salt and pepper** (to taste)

Instructions:

1. **Prepare the Ingredients:**
    - Dice or shred the cooked chicken breast.
    - Cut the pineapple and mango into bite-sized chunks.
    - Dice the red bell pepper and finely chop the red onion.
    - Chop the fresh cilantro and toast the shredded coconut if using.
2. **Make the Dressing:**
    - In a small bowl, whisk together the Greek yogurt, mayonnaise, lime juice, honey, and ground cumin.
    - Season the dressing with salt and pepper to taste.
3. **Combine the Salad:**
    - In a large mixing bowl, combine the cooked chicken, pineapple chunks, mango chunks, red bell pepper, red onion, and chopped cilantro.
    - Gently fold in the dressing until all the ingredients are evenly coated.
4. **Add Nuts and Coconut:**
    - Sprinkle the chopped cashews (or almonds) and shredded coconut (if using) on top of the salad.
5. **Chill and Serve:**
    - Chill the salad in the refrigerator for about 30 minutes before serving to allow the flavors to meld.
    - Serve chilled as a main dish or a side.

Tips:

- **Chicken:** Use leftover roasted or grilled chicken for added flavor, or poach the chicken breast for a simple preparation.
- **Fruits:** For the best flavor, use fresh tropical fruits. If using frozen, make sure they are fully thawed and drained.
- **Customization:** Feel free to add other ingredients like avocado, cucumber, or cherry tomatoes for additional flavor and texture.

Tropical Chicken Salad is a delicious blend of savory, sweet, and tangy flavors that will transport your taste buds to a tropical paradise. Enjoy it as a refreshing lunch or a festive side dish!

Pineapple Upside-Down Cake

Ingredients:

For the Topping:

- **1/4 cup unsalted butter** (1/2 stick)
- **1 cup packed light brown sugar**
- **1 can (20 oz) sliced pineapple** (drained, reserve juice)
- **Maraschino cherries** (about 8-10, drained)

For the Cake Batter:

- **1 1/2 cups all-purpose flour**
- **1 1/2 teaspoons baking powder**
- **1/2 teaspoon baking soda**
- **1/4 teaspoon salt**
- **1/2 cup unsalted butter** (1 stick, softened)
- **1 cup granulated sugar**
- **2 large eggs**
- **1 teaspoon vanilla extract**
- **1/2 cup pineapple juice** (from the canned pineapple)
- **1/2 cup buttermilk** (or milk with a tablespoon of lemon juice)

Instructions:

1. **Prepare the Topping:**
   - Preheat your oven to 350°F (175°C).
   - In a 9-inch round cake pan, melt the 1/4 cup butter in the oven for about 2-3 minutes.
   - Carefully remove the pan from the oven and sprinkle the brown sugar evenly over the melted butter. Stir to combine.
   - Arrange the pineapple slices over the sugar mixture in a single layer. Place a maraschino cherry in the center of each pineapple slice and between the slices if desired.
2. **Prepare the Cake Batter:**
   - In a medium bowl, whisk together the flour, baking powder, baking soda, and salt.
   - In a large bowl, cream together the softened butter and granulated sugar until light and fluffy using an electric mixer.
   - Beat in the eggs one at a time, mixing well after each addition. Stir in the vanilla extract.
   - Gradually add the dry ingredients to the butter mixture, alternating with the pineapple juice and buttermilk. Begin and end with the dry ingredients, mixing just until combined.
   - Pour the batter evenly over the pineapple slices in the cake pan.

3. **Bake the Cake:**
   - Bake in the preheated oven for 40-45 minutes, or until a toothpick inserted into the center of the cake comes out clean and the cake is golden brown.
4. **Cool and Serve:**
   - Allow the cake to cool in the pan for about 10 minutes. Run a knife around the edges of the pan to loosen the cake.
   - Place a serving plate over the pan and carefully invert the cake onto the plate. Let the cake cool completely before serving.
5. **Enjoy:**
   - Serve the cake warm or at room temperature. It's delicious on its own or with a dollop of whipped cream or a scoop of vanilla ice cream.

Tips:

- **Butter:** Make sure the butter is softened for the cake batter to mix evenly.
- **Pineapple Juice:** Use the reserved pineapple juice from the can to enhance the pineapple flavor in the cake.
- **Non-Stick Pan:** If using a non-stick pan, make sure to still use parchment paper or butter and sugar to ensure the cake comes out cleanly.

Pineapple Upside-Down Cake is a timeless dessert that brings together the sweet, tangy flavor of pineapple with a soft, buttery cake. Its impressive presentation and delightful taste make it a favorite for any occasion!

Coconut Shrimp with Sweet Chili Sauce

Ingredients:

For the Coconut Shrimp:

- **1 pound large shrimp** (peeled and deveined, tails on or off as preferred)
- **1/2 cup all-purpose flour**
- **1 teaspoon salt**
- **1/2 teaspoon black pepper**
- **2 large eggs**
- **1 cup shredded coconut** (sweetened or unsweetened, based on preference)
- **1/2 cup panko breadcrumbs** (optional, for extra crunch)
- **Vegetable oil** (for frying)

For the Sweet Chili Sauce:

- **1/2 cup sweet chili sauce** (store-bought or homemade)
- **1 tablespoon lime juice**
- **1 tablespoon fish sauce** (optional, for added depth of flavor)
- **1 teaspoon soy sauce** (optional)
- **1 teaspoon finely chopped fresh cilantro** (optional, for garnish)

Instructions:

1. **Prepare the Shrimp:**
    - If not already done, peel and devein the shrimp, leaving the tails on or off based on your preference.
    - Pat the shrimp dry with paper towels to remove excess moisture. This helps the coating stick better.
2. **Set Up Breading Station:**
    - In a shallow dish, combine the flour, salt, and black pepper.
    - In a second shallow dish, beat the eggs.
    - In a third shallow dish, combine the shredded coconut and panko breadcrumbs (if using).
3. **Coat the Shrimp:**
    - Dredge each shrimp in the flour mixture, shaking off excess.
    - Dip the floured shrimp into the beaten eggs, allowing any excess to drip off.
    - Press the shrimp into the coconut mixture, ensuring they are evenly coated.
4. **Fry the Shrimp:**
    - Heat about 1/2 inch of vegetable oil in a large skillet over medium-high heat until it reaches 350°F (175°C). You can test the oil by dropping in a small piece of bread; if it bubbles and floats, the oil is ready.
    - Fry the shrimp in batches, making sure not to overcrowd the pan. Cook for 2-3 minutes per side, or until the shrimp are golden brown and crispy.

- Use a slotted spoon to transfer the shrimp to a plate lined with paper towels to drain excess oil.
5. **Prepare the Sweet Chili Sauce:**
    - In a small bowl, mix together the sweet chili sauce, lime juice, fish sauce, and soy sauce (if using). Stir until well combined.
    - Garnish with chopped fresh cilantro if desired.
6. **Serve:**
    - Serve the crispy coconut shrimp with the sweet chili sauce on the side for dipping.
    - You can also garnish with extra lime wedges or cilantro if you like.

Tips:

- **Coconut:** Use sweetened shredded coconut for a slightly sweeter flavor, or unsweetened for a more natural taste.
- **Oil Temperature:** Maintaining the correct oil temperature is crucial for achieving crispy shrimp without absorbing too much oil. Adjust the heat as needed.
- **Homemade Sweet Chili Sauce:** If you prefer to make your own sweet chili sauce, combine 1/2 cup sugar, 1/4 cup rice vinegar, 1/4 cup water, 2 tablespoons chili garlic sauce, and a pinch of salt. Simmer until thickened.

Coconut Shrimp with Sweet Chili Sauce offers a delightful combination of crispy, savory, and sweet flavors that are sure to please your taste buds. Enjoy this tropical treat as a satisfying appetizer or a fun main dish!

Barbados Style Flying Fish

Ingredients:

For the Marinade:

- **4-6 flying fish fillets** (cleaned and boned, or you can use another type of fish like snapper if flying fish is not available)
- **2 tablespoons lime juice** (or lemon juice)
- **2 cloves garlic** (minced)
- **1 teaspoon fresh thyme leaves** (or 1/2 teaspoon dried thyme)
- **1 teaspoon paprika**
- **1 teaspoon allspice** (pimento)
- **1/2 teaspoon cayenne pepper** (optional, for added heat)
- **1 teaspoon salt**
- **1/2 teaspoon black pepper**
- **1 tablespoon vegetable oil**

For Frying:

- **Vegetable oil** (for frying)

Instructions:

1. **Marinate the Fish:**
    - Rinse the flying fish fillets under cold water and pat them dry with paper towels.
    - In a bowl, combine the lime juice, minced garlic, thyme, paprika, allspice, cayenne pepper (if using), salt, black pepper, and vegetable oil.
    - Rub the marinade all over the fish fillets, ensuring they are well-coated. Cover and refrigerate for at least 1 hour, or overnight for deeper flavor.
2. **Prepare for Cooking:**
    - Heat about 1/2 inch of vegetable oil in a large skillet over medium-high heat. The oil should be hot but not smoking.
    - If you prefer grilling, preheat your grill to medium-high heat and lightly oil the grill grates.
3. **Cook the Fish:**
    - **Frying:**
        - Once the oil is hot, carefully place the marinated fish fillets into the skillet. Fry for about 2-3 minutes per side, or until the fish is golden brown and cooked through. The fish should easily flake with a fork.
        - Use a slotted spoon or tongs to transfer the fried fish to a plate lined with paper towels to drain excess oil.
    - **Grilling:**

- Place the marinated fish fillets on the preheated grill. Grill for about 4-5 minutes per side, or until the fish is opaque and flakes easily with a fork. Brush with a bit of oil or marinade to prevent sticking.

4. **Serve:**
    - Serve the Barbados Style Flying Fish hot, garnished with fresh lime wedges and additional thyme if desired.
    - This dish pairs wonderfully with traditional sides such as cou-cou, rice and peas, or a simple salad.

Tips:

- **Marinating:** Allowing the fish to marinate for several hours or overnight enhances the flavor, so plan ahead if possible.
- **Oil Temperature:** Make sure the oil is hot before adding the fish to prevent sticking and ensure a crispy texture.
- **Alternative Cooking Methods:** If you prefer a healthier option, you can bake the marinated fish at 375°F (190°C) for about 15-20 minutes, or until cooked through.

Barbados Style Flying Fish captures the essence of Caribbean cuisine with its blend of aromatic spices and fresh flavors. Enjoy this delicious dish as a taste of the island!

Caribbean Black Bean Soup

Ingredients:

- **2 tablespoons vegetable oil**
- **1 large onion** (diced)
- **1 red bell pepper** (diced)
- **3 cloves garlic** (minced)
- **1 carrot** (diced)
- **1 celery stalk** (diced)
- **1 teaspoon ground cumin**
- **1 teaspoon paprika**
- **1/2 teaspoon ground allspice**
- **1/4 teaspoon cayenne pepper** (optional, for heat)
- **2 cans (15 oz each) black beans** (rinsed and drained, or 3 cups cooked black beans)
- **4 cups vegetable or chicken broth**
- **1 can (14.5 oz) diced tomatoes** (with juice)
- **1 bay leaf**
- **1 teaspoon dried thyme** (or 1 tablespoon fresh thyme)
- **1 tablespoon soy sauce** (or tamari for gluten-free)
- **1 tablespoon lime juice** (freshly squeezed)
- **Salt and black pepper** (to taste)
- **1/4 cup fresh cilantro** (chopped, for garnish)
- **1 avocado** (diced, for garnish)
- **Lime wedges** (for serving)

Instructions:

1. **Sauté Vegetables:**
   - Heat the vegetable oil in a large pot over medium heat.
   - Add the diced onion, red bell pepper, garlic, carrot, and celery. Sauté for about 5-7 minutes, or until the vegetables are softened and the onion is translucent.
2. **Add Spices:**
   - Stir in the ground cumin, paprika, allspice, and cayenne pepper (if using). Cook for an additional 1-2 minutes, or until the spices are fragrant.
3. **Add Beans and Liquids:**
   - Add the black beans, vegetable or chicken broth, diced tomatoes with their juice, bay leaf, and dried thyme to the pot.
   - Bring the mixture to a boil, then reduce the heat and let it simmer for about 20-25 minutes, allowing the flavors to meld together.
4. **Blend the Soup (Optional):**
   - For a creamier texture, you can blend part of the soup. Use an immersion blender to puree some of the soup directly in the pot, or transfer 2-3 cups of the soup to a blender, blend until smooth, and return it to the pot.
   - If you prefer a chunkier soup, skip this step.

5. **Season and Finish:**
    - Stir in the soy sauce and lime juice. Season with salt and black pepper to taste.
    - Remove the bay leaf before serving.
6. **Serve:**
    - Ladle the soup into bowls and garnish with fresh chopped cilantro, diced avocado, and extra lime wedges if desired.
    - Serve hot with your choice of side dishes like rice, plantains, or crusty bread.

Tips:

- **Beans:** If using dried black beans, soak them overnight and cook them according to package instructions before adding them to the soup.
- **Spice Level:** Adjust the cayenne pepper to your taste if you prefer a milder or spicier soup.
- **Storage:** Leftovers can be stored in the refrigerator for up to 5 days or frozen for up to 3 months.

Caribbean Black Bean Soup is a satisfying and nutritious dish that brings the vibrant flavors of the Caribbean to your table. Enjoy its hearty and spicy goodness!

Spicy Tamarind Shrimp Tacos

Ingredients:

For the Shrimp:

- **1 pound large shrimp** (peeled and deveined)
- **2 tablespoons tamarind paste**
- **1 tablespoon olive oil**
- **1 teaspoon ground cumin**
- **1 teaspoon smoked paprika**
- **1/2 teaspoon cayenne pepper** (or to taste)
- **1 teaspoon garlic powder**
- **1 teaspoon onion powder**
- **1/2 teaspoon ground coriander**
- **1/2 teaspoon salt**
- **1/4 teaspoon black pepper**

For the Taco Slaw:

- **2 cups shredded cabbage** (green or purple, or a mix)
- **1 carrot** (shredded)
- **1/4 cup chopped fresh cilantro**
- **1 tablespoon lime juice**
- **1 tablespoon honey**
- **1 tablespoon apple cider vinegar**
- **Salt and pepper** (to taste)

For Serving:

- **8 small corn or flour tortillas**
- **1 avocado** (sliced)
- **Lime wedges** (for serving)
- **Sour cream or Greek yogurt** (optional, for garnish)
- **Hot sauce** (optional, for extra heat)

Instructions:

1. **Prepare the Shrimp:**
    - In a bowl, combine the tamarind paste, olive oil, cumin, smoked paprika, cayenne pepper, garlic powder, onion powder, ground coriander, salt, and black pepper.
    - Toss the shrimp in the marinade, ensuring they are well-coated. Let them marinate for at least 15-30 minutes in the refrigerator.
2. **Cook the Shrimp:**
    - Heat a large skillet or grill pan over medium-high heat.

- Add the marinated shrimp and cook for 2-3 minutes per side, or until they are pink and opaque, with a slight char on the edges. Be careful not to overcook.
3. **Prepare the Taco Slaw:**
    - In a large bowl, combine the shredded cabbage, shredded carrot, and chopped cilantro.
    - In a small bowl, whisk together the lime juice, honey, and apple cider vinegar. Pour the dressing over the slaw and toss to coat.
    - Season with salt and pepper to taste.
4. **Warm the Tortillas:**
    - Warm the tortillas in a dry skillet over medium heat, or wrap them in foil and heat in the oven at 350°F (175°C) for about 5-7 minutes.
5. **Assemble the Tacos:**
    - Place a few shrimp on each tortilla.
    - Top with a generous scoop of the taco slaw.
    - Add slices of avocado on top.
    - Garnish with lime wedges and, if desired, a dollop of sour cream or Greek yogurt and a drizzle of hot sauce.
6. **Serve:**
    - Serve the tacos immediately, while the shrimp and tortillas are still warm.

Tips:

- **Tamarind Paste:** Tamarind paste can be found in most grocery stores or Asian markets. If you can't find it, you can substitute with a bit of lime juice or vinegar for acidity, but the flavor will be slightly different.
- **Marinating Time:** Allowing the shrimp to marinate for longer enhances the flavor, but even a short marination time will give good results.
- **Tortilla Options:** Corn tortillas give a traditional Mexican flavor, but flour tortillas are also a great option if you prefer.

These Spicy Tamarind Shrimp Tacos are a delicious blend of spicy, tangy, and fresh flavors, making them a standout choice for any taco night or casual gathering. Enjoy!

Mango Chutney

Ingredients:

- **3 ripe mangoes** (peeled, pitted, and diced)
- **1 medium onion** (finely chopped)
- **1/2 cup brown sugar** (packed)
- **1/2 cup white vinegar**
- **1/4 cup lemon juice** (freshly squeezed)
- **1/4 cup finely chopped ginger** (or 1 tablespoon ground ginger)
- **2 cloves garlic** (minced)
- **1 teaspoon ground cumin**
- **1 teaspoon ground coriander**
- **1/2 teaspoon ground turmeric**
- **1/2 teaspoon ground cinnamon**
- **1/4 teaspoon ground cloves**
- **1/4 teaspoon red pepper flakes** (optional, for heat)
- **1/2 teaspoon salt**
- **1/2 teaspoon black pepper**
- **1/4 cup raisins** (optional, for added sweetness and texture)

Instructions:

1. **Prepare the Ingredients:**
   - Peel, pit, and dice the mangoes. Set aside.
   - Finely chop the onion and mince the garlic.
2. **Cook the Chutney:**
   - In a large saucepan, combine the diced mangoes, chopped onion, brown sugar, white vinegar, and lemon juice.
   - Stir in the ginger, garlic, ground cumin, ground coriander, turmeric, cinnamon, cloves, and red pepper flakes (if using).
   - Bring the mixture to a boil over medium-high heat, stirring occasionally.
3. **Simmer:**
   - Reduce the heat to low and let the chutney simmer for about 30-40 minutes, stirring frequently. The mixture should thicken and reduce, and the mangoes should become tender.
   - If using, stir in the raisins during the last 10 minutes of cooking.
4. **Adjust Seasoning:**
   - Taste the chutney and adjust seasoning with additional salt, pepper, or sugar if needed. If you prefer a spicier chutney, you can add more red pepper flakes.
5. **Cool and Store:**
   - Remove the chutney from heat and let it cool to room temperature.
   - Transfer the cooled chutney to sterilized jars or containers. Store in the refrigerator for up to 2-3 weeks.
6. **Serve:**

- Serve the mango chutney as a condiment with grilled meats, curries, or as a topping for sandwiches and cheeses.

Tips:

- **Ripeness of Mangoes:** Use ripe mangoes for the best flavor and sweetness. Slightly underripe mangoes can also be used for a tangier chutney.
- **Texture:** If you prefer a smoother chutney, you can use an immersion blender to blend the mixture to your desired consistency after cooking.
- **Sterilizing Jars:** If you plan to store the chutney for an extended period, make sure to sterilize the jars and lids to ensure proper preservation.

Mango Chutney is a delightful blend of sweet, tangy, and spicy flavors that can enhance a variety of dishes. Enjoy this homemade chutney as a versatile addition to your culinary repertoire!

Pineapple Cilantro Salsa

Ingredients:

- **1 cup fresh pineapple** (diced)
- **1/2 red onion** (finely chopped)
- **1 small jalapeño** (seeded and finely chopped, optional for heat)
- **1/4 cup fresh cilantro** (chopped)
- **1 tablespoon lime juice** (freshly squeezed)
- **1 tablespoon honey** (or agave nectar)
- **Salt and black pepper** (to taste)

Instructions:

1. **Prepare the Ingredients:**
   - Dice the fresh pineapple into small cubes.
   - Finely chop the red onion and jalapeño (if using).
2. **Mix the Salsa:**
   - In a medium bowl, combine the diced pineapple, chopped red onion, jalapeño, and fresh cilantro.
   - Stir in the lime juice and honey, mixing well to combine all ingredients.
3. **Season:**
   - Season the salsa with salt and black pepper to taste. Adjust the sweetness or acidity if needed by adding a bit more honey or lime juice.
4. **Chill:**
   - For best flavor, let the salsa chill in the refrigerator for at least 30 minutes to allow the flavors to meld.
5. **Serve:**
   - Serve the pineapple cilantro salsa with tortilla chips, as a topping for grilled meats or fish, or as a fresh accompaniment to your favorite dishes.

Tips:

- **Ripeness of Pineapple:** Use ripe pineapple for the best sweetness and flavor. If you prefer a more tart salsa, slightly underripe pineapple works well.
- **Heat Level:** Adjust the amount of jalapeño according to your heat preference, or omit it entirely for a milder salsa.
- **Texture:** For a chunkier salsa, keep the pineapple in larger pieces. For a finer texture, you can chop the pineapple more finely.

Pineapple Cilantro Salsa offers a delightful blend of sweet, tangy, and fresh flavors that can enhance a variety of dishes. Enjoy this refreshing salsa as a versatile addition to your meals!

Plantain and Black Bean Empanadas

Ingredients:

For the Filling:

- **2 ripe plantains** (peeled and diced)
- **1 tablespoon olive oil**
- **1 small onion** (diced)
- **2 cloves garlic** (minced)
- **1 can (15 oz) black beans** (rinsed and drained, or 1.5 cups cooked black beans)
- **1/2 teaspoon ground cumin**
- **1/2 teaspoon smoked paprika**
- **1/2 teaspoon ground coriander**
- **1/4 teaspoon cayenne pepper** (optional, for heat)
- **Salt and black pepper** (to taste)
- **1/4 cup fresh cilantro** (chopped)
- **1/4 cup crumbled feta cheese** (optional, for added richness)

For the Dough:

- **2 1/2 cups all-purpose flour**
- **1/2 teaspoon salt**
- **1/2 teaspoon baking powder**
- **1/2 cup unsalted butter** (cold and cut into small pieces)
- **1 large egg**
- **1/2 cup cold water** (or as needed)

For Assembling:

- **1 egg** (beaten, for egg wash)
- **Flour** (for dusting)

Instructions:

1. **Prepare the Filling:**
    - Heat the olive oil in a large skillet over medium heat. Add the diced onion and cook until translucent, about 5 minutes.
    - Add the minced garlic and cook for another 1-2 minutes, until fragrant.
    - Stir in the diced plantains and cook for about 5-7 minutes, or until they are tender and starting to caramelize.
    - Add the black beans, ground cumin, smoked paprika, ground coriander, and cayenne pepper (if using). Cook for another 2-3 minutes, allowing the flavors to meld. Season with salt and black pepper to taste.
    - Remove from heat and stir in the chopped cilantro and crumbled feta cheese (if using). Let the filling cool.

2. **Prepare the Dough:**
    - In a large bowl, whisk together the flour, salt, and baking powder.
    - Cut the cold butter into the flour mixture using a pastry cutter or your fingers until the mixture resembles coarse crumbs.
    - In a separate bowl, beat the egg and then stir it into the flour mixture.
    - Gradually add cold water, a little at a time, until the dough comes together. It should be soft but not sticky.
    - Turn the dough out onto a floured surface and knead briefly until smooth. Wrap in plastic wrap and refrigerate for at least 30 minutes.
3. **Assemble the Empanadas:**
    - Preheat your oven to 375°F (190°C). Line a baking sheet with parchment paper.
    - On a lightly floured surface, roll out the dough to about 1/8-inch thickness. Use a round cutter (about 4-5 inches in diameter) to cut out circles of dough.
    - Place a spoonful of the plantain and black bean filling in the center of each dough circle.
    - Fold the dough over the filling to create a half-moon shape. Press the edges together to seal, then crimp the edges with a fork to ensure they are well-sealed.
    - Brush the tops of the empanadas with the beaten egg for a golden finish.
4. **Bake:**
    - Place the empanadas on the prepared baking sheet.
    - Bake for 20-25 minutes, or until the empanadas are golden brown and the dough is crisp.
5. **Serve:**
    - Allow the empanadas to cool slightly before serving. They can be enjoyed warm or at room temperature.

Tips:

- **Plantain Ripeness:** Use ripe plantains for a sweeter filling. If they are too ripe, they might become mushy, so look for plantains that are just ripe.
- **Freezing:** These empanadas freeze well. Assemble them and freeze them before baking. When ready to bake, bake from frozen, adding a few extra minutes to the cooking time.
- **Variations:** You can add other ingredients to the filling, such as diced bell peppers or corn, to suit your taste.

Plantain and Black Bean Empanadas are a flavorful and satisfying dish that combines sweet and savory elements in a convenient handheld format. Enjoy!

Grilled Swordfish with Citrus Salsa

Ingredients:

For the Swordfish:

- **4 swordfish steaks** (about 6 ounces each)
- **2 tablespoons olive oil**
- **1 teaspoon paprika**
- **1 teaspoon garlic powder**
- **1/2 teaspoon dried oregano**
- **Salt and black pepper** (to taste)
- **Lemon wedges** (for serving)

For the Citrus Salsa:

- **1 large orange** (peeled and segmented)
- **1 large grapefruit** (peeled and segmented)
- **1/2 red onion** (finely chopped)
- **1 small jalapeño** (seeded and finely chopped, optional for heat)
- **1/4 cup fresh cilantro** (chopped)
- **1 tablespoon lime juice** (freshly squeezed)
- **1 tablespoon honey** (or agave nectar)
- **Salt and black pepper** (to taste)

Instructions:

1. **Prepare the Swordfish:**
    - Preheat your grill to medium-high heat.
    - In a small bowl, combine the olive oil, paprika, garlic powder, dried oregano, salt, and black pepper.
    - Brush the swordfish steaks with the seasoned olive oil mixture on both sides.
2. **Grill the Swordfish:**
    - Place the swordfish steaks on the grill and cook for 4-5 minutes per side, or until the fish is opaque and easily flakes with a fork. The exact cooking time may vary depending on the thickness of the steaks.
    - Remove the swordfish from the grill and let it rest for a few minutes before serving.
3. **Prepare the Citrus Salsa:**
    - In a medium bowl, combine the orange and grapefruit segments, red onion, and jalapeño (if using).
    - Stir in the chopped cilantro, lime juice, and honey. Mix well to combine.
    - Season the salsa with salt and black pepper to taste.
4. **Serve:**
    - Place the grilled swordfish steaks on serving plates.

- Spoon the citrus salsa over the top of each steak.
- Serve with lemon wedges on the side.

Tips:

- **Swordfish:** Look for swordfish steaks that are firm and have a fresh, clean smell. Swordfish is a meaty fish that holds up well on the grill.
- **Citrus Salsa:** Feel free to adjust the citrus fruits in the salsa according to what's available or your taste preferences. Other fruits like tangerines or blood oranges can be good alternatives.
- **Make Ahead:** You can prepare the citrus salsa ahead of time and refrigerate it until you're ready to serve. Just give it a good stir before using.

Grilled Swordfish with Citrus Salsa is a light yet flavorful meal that brings together the richness of swordfish with the bright, tangy flavors of citrus. Enjoy this dish for a perfect blend of taste and freshness!

Island Style Beef Kebabs

Ingredients:

For the Marinade:

- 1/4 cup soy sauce
- 1/4 cup orange juice (freshly squeezed)
- 2 tablespoons lime juice (freshly squeezed)
- 2 tablespoons brown sugar
- 2 tablespoons olive oil
- 2 cloves garlic (minced)
- 1 tablespoon fresh ginger (grated)
- 1 teaspoon ground allspice
- 1 teaspoon paprika
- 1/2 teaspoon ground cumin
- 1/2 teaspoon dried thyme
- 1/4 teaspoon cayenne pepper (optional, for heat)
- Salt and black pepper (to taste)

For the Kebabs:

- 1.5 pounds beef sirloin or flank steak (cut into 1.5-inch cubes)
- 1 red bell pepper (cut into chunks)
- 1 green bell pepper (cut into chunks)
- 1 onion (cut into chunks)
- 1 zucchini (sliced into thick rounds)
- 1 cup cherry tomatoes

For Garnish (Optional):

- Fresh cilantro (chopped)
- Lime wedges

Instructions:

1. **Prepare the Marinade:**
   - In a medium bowl, whisk together the soy sauce, orange juice, lime juice, brown sugar, olive oil, minced garlic, grated ginger, allspice, paprika, ground cumin, dried thyme, cayenne pepper (if using), salt, and black pepper.
   - Taste and adjust seasoning if needed.
2. **Marinate the Beef:**
   - Place the beef cubes in a large resealable plastic bag or shallow dish.
   - Pour the marinade over the beef, ensuring all pieces are well coated.
   - Seal the bag or cover the dish and refrigerate for at least 1 hour, or up to 8 hours for more intense flavor.

3. **Prepare the Vegetables:**
   - While the beef is marinating, prepare the vegetables by cutting them into chunks that are similar in size to the beef cubes.
4. **Assemble the Kebabs:**
   - Preheat your grill to medium-high heat.
   - Thread the marinated beef cubes and vegetables onto skewers, alternating between beef and vegetables. If using wooden skewers, soak them in water for at least 30 minutes before using to prevent burning.
5. **Grill the Kebabs:**
   - Place the skewers on the grill and cook for about 8-12 minutes, turning occasionally, until the beef is cooked to your desired level of doneness and the vegetables are tender and slightly charred.
   - For medium-rare beef, cook to an internal temperature of 135°F (57°C). Adjust grilling time as needed for your preferred doneness.
6. **Serve:**
   - Remove the kebabs from the grill and let them rest for a few minutes.
   - Garnish with fresh cilantro and serve with lime wedges on the side for squeezing over the kebabs.

Tips:

- **Beef Cuts:** Sirloin or flank steak works well for kebabs because they are tender and flavorful. Make sure to cut the beef into uniform pieces for even cooking.
- **Marinating Time:** Marinating the beef for a longer period enhances the flavor. If you're short on time, even a 1-hour marinade will still be delicious.
- **Grill Temperature:** Medium-high heat is ideal for getting a good sear on the beef and vegetables while cooking them through.

Island Style Beef Kebabs offer a delicious blend of sweet, tangy, and savory flavors with a touch of tropical flair. They're perfect for a summer barbecue or any time you want to bring a bit of island flavor to your meal. Enjoy!

Tropical Banana Bread

Ingredients:

- **1 1/2 cups all-purpose flour**
- **1/2 teaspoon baking powder**
- **1/2 teaspoon baking soda**
- **1/4 teaspoon salt**
- **1/2 teaspoon ground cinnamon**
- **1/4 teaspoon ground nutmeg** (optional)
- **1/2 cup unsalted butter** (softened)
- **1/2 cup granulated sugar**
- **1/4 cup packed brown sugar**
- **2 large eggs**
- **3 ripe bananas** (mashed, about 1 1/2 cups)
- **1/2 cup crushed pineapple** (drained)
- **1/2 cup shredded coconut**
- **1/4 cup chopped walnuts or pecans** (optional)
- **1/4 cup dried shredded coconut** (for topping, optional)

Instructions:

1. **Prepare the Oven and Pan:**
   - Preheat your oven to 350°F (175°C).
   - Grease and flour a 9x5-inch loaf pan or line it with parchment paper.
2. **Mix the Dry Ingredients:**
   - In a medium bowl, whisk together the flour, baking powder, baking soda, salt, cinnamon, and nutmeg (if using).
3. **Cream the Butter and Sugars:**
   - In a large bowl, using an electric mixer, cream together the softened butter, granulated sugar, and brown sugar until light and fluffy.
4. **Add the Eggs and Bananas:**
   - Beat in the eggs one at a time, mixing well after each addition.
   - Stir in the mashed bananas until well combined.
5. **Combine the Ingredients:**
   - Gradually add the dry ingredients to the banana mixture, mixing just until combined.
   - Gently fold in the crushed pineapple, shredded coconut, and chopped walnuts or pecans (if using).
6. **Pour and Bake:**
   - Pour the batter into the prepared loaf pan.
   - Sprinkle the top with dried shredded coconut, if desired.
   - Bake in the preheated oven for 60-70 minutes, or until a toothpick inserted into the center of the loaf comes out clean.
7. **Cool and Serve:**

- Allow the bread to cool in the pan for 10 minutes, then transfer to a wire rack to cool completely before slicing.

Tips:

- **Ripeness of Bananas:** Use very ripe bananas for the best flavor and sweetness. Overripe bananas work best because they are softer and sweeter.
- **Draining Pineapple:** Make sure to drain the pineapple well to avoid excess moisture in the batter.
- **Storage:** Store the banana bread in an airtight container at room temperature for up to 4 days. For longer storage, wrap it tightly in plastic wrap and freeze for up to 3 months.

Tropical Banana Bread brings a taste of the tropics to your kitchen with the addition of coconut and pineapple. It's a delicious and unique variation of the classic banana bread that's sure to be a hit with everyone!

Coconut Milk and Pineapple Popsicles

Ingredients:

- **1 can (13.5 oz) full-fat coconut milk**
- **1 cup fresh pineapple** (diced, or use frozen pineapple chunks)
- **1/4 cup honey** (or maple syrup, adjust to taste)
- **1 tablespoon lime juice** (freshly squeezed)
- **1/2 teaspoon vanilla extract** (optional)
- **Pinch of salt** (optional, to enhance flavor)

Instructions:

1. **Prepare the Pineapple:**
   - If using fresh pineapple, peel and cut it into chunks. If using frozen pineapple, let it thaw slightly for easier blending.
2. **Blend the Ingredients:**
   - In a blender or food processor, combine the pineapple chunks, honey (or maple syrup), lime juice, vanilla extract (if using), and a pinch of salt (if desired). Blend until smooth.
3. **Mix with Coconut Milk:**
   - Pour the coconut milk into the blender with the pineapple mixture. Blend again until everything is well combined.
4. **Pour into Molds:**
   - Pour the mixture into popsicle molds, leaving a small space at the top for expansion.
   - Insert sticks into the molds. If you don't have popsicle sticks, you can use small plastic spoons or simply freeze the mixture in small paper cups with toothpicks.
5. **Freeze:**
   - Place the molds in the freezer and freeze for at least 4 hours, or until completely frozen.
6. **Unmold and Serve:**
   - To release the popsicles from the molds, run warm water over the outside of the molds for a few seconds to loosen them. Gently pull on the sticks to remove the popsicles.
   - Serve immediately or store in a sealed container in the freezer for up to 2 weeks.

Tips:

- **Adjust Sweetness:** Taste the mixture before freezing and adjust the sweetness if needed by adding more honey or maple syrup.
- **Flavor Variations:** You can add a layer of pureed fruit or a swirl of fruit puree to the popsicles before freezing for a fun visual effect and extra flavor.
- **Molds:** If you don't have popsicle molds, silicone ice cube trays or small paper cups work well for making mini popsicles.

These Coconut Milk and Pineapple Popsicles are a tropical delight that's easy to make and perfect for cooling off on a hot day. Enjoy this creamy, fruity treat!

Jamaican Beef Patties

Ingredients:

For the Dough:

- 2 1/2 cups **all-purpose flour**
- 1 teaspoon **baking powder**
- 1/2 teaspoon **salt**
- 1/2 teaspoon **turmeric** (for color and flavor)
- 1/2 cup **unsalted butter** (cold and cut into small pieces)
- 1/2 cup **shortening** (cold, or you can use more butter)
- 1/4 cup **ice water** (plus more if needed)

For the Beef Filling:

- 1 **tablespoon vegetable oil**
- 1 **small onion** (finely chopped)
- 2 **cloves garlic** (minced)
- 1 **pound ground beef**
- 1/2 teaspoon **ground allspice**
- 1/2 teaspoon **ground paprika**
- 1/2 teaspoon **ground cumin**
- 1/2 teaspoon **dried thyme**
- 1/4 teaspoon **cayenne pepper** (adjust to taste for heat)
- 1 **tablespoon soy sauce**
- 1/2 cup **beef broth**
- 1/2 cup **breadcrumbs** (or cooked rice for a different texture)
- **Salt and black pepper** (to taste)
- 1/4 cup **fresh cilantro** (chopped, optional)

For Assembly:

- 1 **egg** (beaten, for egg wash)

Instructions:

1. **Prepare the Dough:**
   - In a large bowl, whisk together the flour, baking powder, salt, and turmeric.
   - Cut in the cold butter and shortening using a pastry cutter or your fingers until the mixture resembles coarse crumbs.
   - Gradually add the ice water, a tablespoon at a time, until the dough comes together. Be careful not to add too much water; the dough should be soft but not sticky.
   - Gather the dough into a ball, wrap it in plastic wrap, and refrigerate for at least 30 minutes.

2. **Prepare the Beef Filling:**
    - Heat the vegetable oil in a large skillet over medium heat. Add the chopped onion and cook until softened, about 5 minutes.
    - Add the minced garlic and cook for another minute.
    - Add the ground beef and cook until browned, breaking it up with a spoon.
    - Stir in the allspice, paprika, cumin, thyme, and cayenne pepper. Cook for 2-3 minutes until the spices are well combined with the beef.
    - Add the soy sauce and beef broth, stirring to combine. Let the mixture simmer for 5-7 minutes until most of the liquid has evaporated.
    - Stir in the breadcrumbs (or cooked rice) and cook for an additional 2 minutes. Season with salt and black pepper to taste.
    - Remove from heat and let the filling cool. Stir in the chopped cilantro if using.
3. **Assemble the Patties:**
    - Preheat your oven to 375°F (190°C) and line a baking sheet with parchment paper.
    - On a lightly floured surface, roll out the dough to about 1/8-inch thickness.
    - Cut out circles of dough using a 4-5 inch round cutter.
    - Place a spoonful of the beef filling in the center of each dough circle.
    - Fold the dough over the filling to create a half-moon shape. Press the edges together to seal, then crimp the edges with a fork to ensure they are well-sealed.
    - Brush the tops of the patties with the beaten egg for a golden finish.
4. **Bake:**
    - Place the patties on the prepared baking sheet.
    - Bake in the preheated oven for 25-30 minutes, or until the patties are golden brown and the dough is cooked through.
5. **Serve:**
    - Allow the patties to cool slightly before serving. They can be enjoyed warm or at room temperature.

Tips:

- **Dough Consistency:** The dough should be chilled to make it easier to handle and to ensure a flaky texture. If the dough becomes too soft while rolling out, return it to the refrigerator for a few minutes.
- **Spice Level:** Adjust the amount of cayenne pepper to suit your heat preference. You can also experiment with other spices like Scotch bonnet pepper for a more authentic kick.
- **Freezing:** Jamaican Beef Patties freeze well. To freeze, assemble and bake them, then let them cool completely before wrapping them individually in plastic wrap and freezing. Reheat in a 350°F (175°C) oven for 10-15 minutes.

Enjoy these delicious and flavorful Jamaican Beef Patties as a taste of the Caribbean!

Sweet and Sour Mango Chicken

Ingredients:

For the Chicken:

- **1 pound boneless, skinless chicken breasts** (cut into bite-sized pieces)
- **Salt and black pepper** (to taste)
- **1 tablespoon vegetable oil** (or any neutral oil for cooking)

For the Sweet and Sour Sauce:

- **1 cup fresh mango** (peeled and diced, or use frozen mango chunks)
- **1/4 cup rice vinegar**
- **1/4 cup soy sauce**
- **1/4 cup honey** (or maple syrup)
- **2 tablespoons ketchup**
- **2 tablespoons cornstarch**
- **1/2 cup water**
- **1 clove garlic** (minced)
- **1 teaspoon fresh ginger** (grated)
- **1/2 teaspoon red pepper flakes** (optional, for heat)
- **1/4 teaspoon salt** (to taste)

For Garnish (Optional):

- **Chopped fresh cilantro**
- **Sesame seeds**
- **Sliced green onions**

Instructions:

1. **Prepare the Chicken:**
   - Season the chicken pieces with salt and black pepper.
   - Heat the vegetable oil in a large skillet or wok over medium-high heat.
   - Add the chicken pieces and cook until browned and cooked through, about 5-7 minutes. Remove the chicken from the skillet and set aside.
2. **Make the Sweet and Sour Sauce:**
   - In a blender or food processor, combine the diced mango, rice vinegar, soy sauce, honey, ketchup, garlic, ginger, and red pepper flakes (if using). Blend until smooth.
   - In a small bowl, mix the cornstarch with water to make a slurry.
   - Pour the mango mixture into the skillet or wok and bring to a simmer over medium heat.
   - Stir in the cornstarch slurry and continue to simmer until the sauce thickens, about 2-3 minutes. Taste and adjust seasoning with salt if needed.

3. **Combine Chicken and Sauce:**
   - Return the cooked chicken to the skillet or wok, tossing to coat the chicken evenly with the sauce.
   - Cook for an additional 2-3 minutes to heat the chicken through and allow the flavors to meld.
4. **Serve:**
   - Transfer the Sweet and Sour Mango Chicken to serving plates.
   - Garnish with chopped cilantro, sesame seeds, and sliced green onions if desired.
   - Serve over rice, quinoa, or with steamed vegetables.

Tips:

- **Mango:** Fresh mango is ideal, but if you use frozen mango, make sure to thaw it before blending.
- **Sauce Consistency:** If you prefer a thicker sauce, add a bit more cornstarch slurry. If the sauce is too thick, add a splash of water to reach the desired consistency.
- **Chicken Alternatives:** You can use chicken thighs instead of breasts for a richer flavor. Just be sure to adjust the cooking time as needed.

Sweet and Sour Mango Chicken offers a delightful combination of tropical sweetness and savory tang, making it a hit for both family dinners and special occasions. Enjoy!

Grilled Calamari with Lime Dressing

Ingredients:

For the Calamari:

- **1 pound fresh calamari** (cleaned, with tentacles separated and bodies sliced into rings)
- **2 tablespoons olive oil**
- **1 teaspoon smoked paprika** (or regular paprika)
- **1/2 teaspoon garlic powder**
- **Salt and black pepper** (to taste)
- **1 lemon** (cut into wedges, for serving)

For the Lime Dressing:

- **1/4 cup freshly squeezed lime juice** (about 2 limes)
- **2 tablespoons extra virgin olive oil**
- **1 tablespoon honey** (or agave syrup for a vegan option)
- **1 clove garlic** (minced)
- **1/2 teaspoon ground cumin**
- **1/4 teaspoon red pepper flakes** (optional, for heat)
- **Salt and black pepper** (to taste)
- **2 tablespoons chopped fresh cilantro** (optional, for garnish)

Instructions:

1. **Prepare the Calamari:**
   - Rinse the calamari under cold water and pat dry with paper towels.
   - In a large bowl, toss the calamari with olive oil, smoked paprika, garlic powder, salt, and black pepper until evenly coated.
2. **Preheat the Grill:**
   - Preheat your grill to high heat (around 450°F or 230°C). If using a grill pan, preheat it over medium-high heat.
3. **Grill the Calamari:**
   - Place the calamari on the grill or grill pan in a single layer. Cook for 2-3 minutes per side, or until the calamari is opaque and has nice grill marks. Avoid overcooking, as calamari can become tough if grilled too long.
   - Remove from the grill and transfer to a serving plate.
4. **Prepare the Lime Dressing:**
   - In a small bowl, whisk together the lime juice, olive oil, honey, minced garlic, ground cumin, red pepper flakes (if using), salt, and black pepper until well combined.
   - Taste and adjust seasoning as needed.
5. **Serve:**
   - Drizzle the lime dressing over the grilled calamari.

- Garnish with chopped fresh cilantro if desired.
- Serve immediately with lemon wedges on the side.

Tips:

- **Grilling Time:** Calamari cooks quickly. Keep an eye on it to ensure it doesn't overcook and become rubbery.
- **Marinating:** For extra flavor, you can marinate the calamari in the olive oil, paprika, and garlic powder for 30 minutes before grilling.
- **Serving Suggestions:** This dish pairs well with a fresh salad, rice, or a side of grilled vegetables.

Grilled Calamari with Lime Dressing is a vibrant and refreshing dish that highlights the delicate flavors of calamari with a tangy and sweet dressing. Enjoy this easy-to-make recipe for a taste of the coast!

Pineapple and Coconut Smoothie Bowl

Ingredients:

For the Smoothie Base:

- **1 cup fresh pineapple chunks** (or frozen for a thicker consistency)
- **1/2 cup coconut milk** (canned or carton, for a creamier texture use canned)
- **1/2 cup plain Greek yogurt** (or coconut yogurt for a dairy-free option)
- **1 banana** (peeled and sliced, preferably frozen for a thicker consistency)
- **1 tablespoon honey** (or maple syrup for a vegan option)
- **1/2 teaspoon vanilla extract** (optional)
- **1/4 cup shredded coconut** (optional, for extra coconut flavor)

For Toppings:

- **Sliced fresh fruit** (such as strawberries, kiwi, or additional pineapple)
- **Granola**
- **Chia seeds or flaxseeds**
- **Nuts** (such as almonds or cashews)
- **Fresh mint leaves** (optional, for garnish)
- **Additional shredded coconut**

Instructions:

1. **Prepare the Smoothie Base:**
   - In a blender, combine the pineapple chunks, coconut milk, Greek yogurt, banana, honey, and vanilla extract.
   - Blend until smooth and creamy. If the mixture is too thick, you can add a bit more coconut milk to reach your desired consistency. For a thicker bowl, use frozen pineapple and banana.
2. **Assemble the Smoothie Bowl:**
   - Pour the smoothie mixture into a bowl.
3. **Add Toppings:**
   - Arrange your chosen toppings on the smoothie. Start with fresh fruit slices, then add granola, chia seeds, nuts, and a sprinkle of shredded coconut.
   - Garnish with fresh mint leaves if desired.
4. **Serve:**
   - Enjoy immediately with a spoon for a satisfying and nutritious meal.

Tips:

- **Texture Adjustments:** For a thicker smoothie bowl, use frozen pineapple and banana. For a thinner consistency, add a bit more coconut milk or a splash of water.

- **Sweetness Level:** Adjust the sweetness to your preference by varying the amount of honey or adding a bit more fruit if needed.
- **Topping Variations:** Feel free to experiment with different toppings like cacao nibs, goji berries, or nut butters.

This Pineapple and Coconut Smoothie Bowl is a delightful way to start your day or to enjoy as a refreshing treat. It's packed with tropical flavors and can be customized with your favorite toppings for a personalized touch!

Caribbean Spiced Rice

Ingredients:

- **1 cup long-grain white rice** (or basmati rice for a slightly different texture)
- **2 tablespoons vegetable oil** (or coconut oil for extra flavor)
- **1 small onion** (finely chopped)
- **2 cloves garlic** (minced)
- **1 bell pepper** (diced, any color)
- **1 small carrot** (diced)
- **1 teaspoon ground allspice**
- **1/2 teaspoon ground cumin**
- **1/2 teaspoon paprika**
- **1/4 teaspoon ground turmeric** (for color)
- **1/4 teaspoon cayenne pepper** (optional, for heat)
- **1 teaspoon dried thyme**
- **1/2 teaspoon salt** (or to taste)
- **1/4 teaspoon black pepper**
- **1 3/4 cups chicken broth** (or vegetable broth for a vegetarian option)
- **1/2 cup coconut milk** (canned or carton)
- **1/2 cup frozen peas** (optional, for added color and flavor)
- **2 tablespoons chopped fresh cilantro** (for garnish)
- **Lime wedges** (for serving)

Instructions:

1. **Prepare the Rice:**
    - Rinse the rice under cold water until the water runs clear. This helps to remove excess starch and prevents the rice from being overly sticky.
2. **Sauté the Vegetables:**
    - In a medium pot or saucepan, heat the vegetable oil over medium heat.
    - Add the chopped onion, garlic, bell pepper, and carrot. Sauté for about 5 minutes, or until the vegetables are softened and the onion is translucent.
3. **Add Spices:**
    - Stir in the ground allspice, cumin, paprika, turmeric, cayenne pepper (if using), dried thyme, salt, and black pepper. Cook for another 1-2 minutes to toast the spices and release their flavors.
4. **Cook the Rice:**
    - Add the rinsed rice to the pot, stirring to coat the rice with the spice mixture.
    - Pour in the chicken broth and coconut milk, stirring to combine. Bring the mixture to a boil.
5. **Simmer:**
    - Reduce the heat to low, cover the pot with a tight-fitting lid, and simmer for 18-20 minutes, or until the rice is cooked and the liquid is absorbed. Avoid stirring the rice during this time to prevent it from becoming mushy.

6. **Finish:**
    - If using frozen peas, stir them into the rice during the last 5 minutes of cooking to heat through.
    - Once the rice is done, remove the pot from heat and let it sit, covered, for 5 minutes. Fluff the rice with a fork to separate the grains.
7. **Garnish and Serve:**
    - Stir in the chopped fresh cilantro.
    - Serve the Caribbean Spiced Rice with lime wedges on the side for an extra burst of flavor.

Tips:

- **Vegetable Variations:** Feel free to add other vegetables like corn, green beans, or diced tomatoes for added flavor and texture.
- **Spice Level:** Adjust the amount of cayenne pepper to control the heat level of the rice.
- **Rice Cooker:** This recipe can also be adapted for a rice cooker. Follow the same steps for sautéing and add the rice, spices, broth, and coconut milk to the rice cooker. Use the "white rice" setting and let it cook until done.

This Caribbean Spiced Rice is a delicious and vibrant side dish that brings a taste of the tropics to your table. Enjoy it with your favorite Caribbean-inspired meals!

Passion Fruit Mojito

Ingredients:

- **1/2 cup fresh passion fruit juice** (or 2-3 fresh passion fruits, halved and seeds scooped out)
- **1/4 cup fresh lime juice** (about 2 limes)
- **2 tablespoons simple syrup** (adjust to taste)
- **10-12 fresh mint leaves** (plus extra for garnish)
- **2 ounces white rum**
- **Club soda** (to top off)
- **Ice**
- **Lime wedges** (for garnish)
- **Passion fruit slices** (optional, for garnish)

Instructions:

1. **Prepare the Passion Fruit Juice:**
   - If using fresh passion fruit, scoop the pulp and seeds into a bowl. Use a spoon to press the pulp through a fine-mesh strainer to extract the juice. You should have about 1/2 cup of juice. Discard the seeds.
2. **Muddle the Mint:**
   - In a glass or cocktail shaker, muddle the mint leaves with the simple syrup and lime juice. Use a muddler or the back of a spoon to gently crush the mint leaves, releasing their oils and flavor.
3. **Add Passion Fruit Juice and Rum:**
   - Add the passion fruit juice and white rum to the glass or shaker. Stir or shake well to combine all the ingredients.
4. **Fill with Ice:**
   - Fill a highball or rocks glass with ice.
5. **Pour and Top Off:**
   - Strain the mixture into the prepared glass over the ice. Top off with club soda, giving it a gentle stir to combine.
6. **Garnish and Serve:**
   - Garnish with a few mint leaves, lime wedges, and passion fruit slices if desired.
   - Serve immediately and enjoy!

Tips:

- **Simple Syrup:** To make simple syrup, combine equal parts sugar and water in a saucepan. Heat over medium heat until the sugar is dissolved. Allow to cool before using. You can also use honey or agave syrup as a substitute.
- **Mint Muddling:** Be gentle when muddling the mint; you want to release the oils without tearing the leaves into small pieces.

- **Passion Fruit Juice:** If fresh passion fruit is not available, you can use store-bought passion fruit juice. Just make sure it's 100% juice for the best flavor.

The Passion Fruit Mojito is a delightful and vibrant cocktail that combines the classic elements of a Mojito with the exotic and refreshing flavor of passion fruit. Enjoy this tropical treat!

Pineapple Basil Sorbet

Ingredients:

- **4 cups fresh pineapple chunks** (about 1 medium pineapple, peeled and cored)
- **1/2 cup fresh basil leaves** (packed)
- **3/4 cup sugar** (adjust to taste; you can use honey or another sweetener if preferred)
- **1/2 cup water**
- **2 tablespoons freshly squeezed lime juice** (about 1 lime)
- **1/2 teaspoon vanilla extract** (optional)
- **Pinch of salt**

Instructions:

1. **Prepare the Pineapple:**
   - If you haven't already, peel, core, and cut the pineapple into chunks.
2. **Blend the Ingredients:**
   - In a blender or food processor, combine the pineapple chunks, basil leaves, sugar, and water. Blend until smooth and well combined.
3. **Strain the Mixture:**
   - To ensure a smooth sorbet, strain the mixture through a fine-mesh sieve into a large bowl to remove any fibrous bits or basil pieces.
4. **Add Lime Juice and Vanilla:**
   - Stir in the lime juice and vanilla extract (if using). Taste the mixture and adjust the sweetness if needed by adding more sugar or sweetener.
5. **Chill the Mixture:**
   - Cover the bowl and refrigerate the mixture for at least 1 hour, or until it is well chilled.
6. **Churn the Sorbet:**
   - Pour the chilled mixture into an ice cream maker and churn according to the manufacturer's instructions, usually for about 20-30 minutes, until the sorbet reaches a smooth and creamy consistency.
7. **Freeze:**
   - Transfer the churned sorbet to an airtight container and freeze for at least 2 hours to firm up further.
8. **Serve:**
   - Scoop the sorbet into bowls or glasses. Garnish with a fresh basil leaf if desired.

Tips:

- **No Ice Cream Maker?** If you don't have an ice cream maker, you can pour the mixture into a shallow dish and freeze it. Every 30 minutes, stir the mixture with a fork to break up ice crystals, until the sorbet is frozen and fluffy (about 3-4 hours).

- **Adjust Sweetness:** Depending on the sweetness of your pineapple, you might need to adjust the amount of sugar. Taste the mixture before freezing to ensure it's sweet enough for your preference.
- **Basil:** If you prefer a subtler basil flavor, you can use fewer basil leaves or reduce the amount added.

Pineapple Basil Sorbet is a refreshing and unique dessert that combines tropical flavors with a hint of herbal sophistication. Enjoy this treat as a light and fruity end to any meal!

Plantain Chips with Avocado Dip

Ingredients:

- **2 ripe but firm plantains** (not overly ripe; they should be yellow with some green)
- **2-3 tablespoons vegetable oil** (or coconut oil for extra flavor)
- **Salt** (to taste)
- **Optional: Paprika, garlic powder, or chili powder** (for added flavor)

Instructions:

1. **Prepare the Plantains:**
   - Peel the plantains and slice them thinly. Aim for slices about 1/8 inch thick. You can use a mandoline slicer for uniform slices.
2. **Heat the Oil:**
   - Heat the vegetable oil in a large skillet or frying pan over medium heat. You need enough oil to cover the bottom of the pan, about 1/4 inch deep.
3. **Fry the Plantain Slices:**
   - Fry the plantain slices in batches, being careful not to overcrowd the pan. Fry for 2-3 minutes per side, or until the chips are golden brown and crispy.
4. **Drain and Season:**
   - Remove the chips with a slotted spoon and transfer them to a plate lined with paper towels to drain excess oil. While still warm, season with salt and any additional spices you like.
5. **Cool:**
   - Let the chips cool completely before serving. They will continue to crisp up as they cool.

Avocado Dip

Ingredients:

- **2 ripe avocados** (peeled, pitted, and mashed)
- **1/4 cup finely chopped red onion**
- **1 small tomato** (diced)
- **1 jalapeño pepper** (seeded and finely chopped, optional for heat)
- **2 tablespoons freshly squeezed lime juice** (about 1 lime)
- **1 clove garlic** (minced)
- **2 tablespoons chopped fresh cilantro**
- **Salt and black pepper** (to taste)

Instructions:

1. **Combine Ingredients:**
   - In a medium bowl, combine the mashed avocados, red onion, tomato, jalapeño pepper (if using), lime juice, minced garlic, and chopped cilantro.
2. **Mix Well:**
   - Stir everything together until well combined. Taste and adjust seasoning with salt and black pepper as needed.
3. **Chill:**
   - For the best flavor, cover the dip and let it chill in the refrigerator for at least 30 minutes before serving.
4. **Serve:**
   - Serve the avocado dip alongside the plantain chips.

Tips:

- **Ripeness:** Make sure the plantains are ripe but still firm. Overripe plantains will be too soft and might become mushy when fried.
- **Crispiness:** Store the plantain chips in an airtight container to keep them crisp. They are best enjoyed fresh but can be stored for a few days.
- **Customization:** Feel free to customize the avocado dip by adding ingredients like diced red bell pepper, a touch of cumin, or a dash of hot sauce for extra kick.

Plantain Chips with Avocado Dip is a delightful combination of textures and flavors, offering a crispy snack paired with a creamy, tangy dip. Enjoy this versatile and delicious duo at your next gathering or as a satisfying snack!

Key Lime Curd Tarts

Ingredients:

- **1 1/2 cups all-purpose flour**
- **1/4 cup granulated sugar**
- **1/2 cup unsalted butter** (cold and cut into small pieces)
- **1 large egg yolk**
- **1-2 tablespoons ice water** (as needed)

Instructions:

1. **Preheat the Oven:**
    - Preheat your oven to 350°F (175°C).
2. **Prepare the Dough:**
    - In a food processor, combine the flour and sugar. Add the cold butter and pulse until the mixture resembles coarse crumbs.
    - Add the egg yolk and pulse to combine. Gradually add ice water, one tablespoon at a time, until the dough begins to come together.
3. **Form the Tart Shells:**
    - Turn the dough out onto a lightly floured surface and gently knead until it forms a cohesive dough. Divide the dough into 6-8 portions and press each portion into the bottom and up the sides of tartlet pans or a muffin tin.
    - Prick the bottoms of the tart shells with a fork to prevent bubbling.
4. **Blind Bake:**
    - Line the tart shells with parchment paper and fill with pie weights or dried beans. Bake for 12-15 minutes, or until the edges are lightly golden. Remove the parchment and weights, and bake for an additional 3-5 minutes until fully golden.
5. **Cool:**
    - Let the tart shells cool completely before filling.

Key Lime Curd

Ingredients:

- **1/2 cup freshly squeezed key lime juice** (about 10-12 key limes or use regular lime juice if key limes are unavailable)
- **1 tablespoon lime zest**
- **1/2 cup granulated sugar**
- **3 large eggs**
- **1/4 cup unsalted butter** (cut into small pieces)
- **Pinch of salt**

Instructions:

1. **Prepare the Curd:**
    - In a heatproof bowl set over a pot of simmering water (double boiler), whisk together the lime juice, lime zest, sugar, and eggs.
2. **Cook the Curd:**
    - Cook the mixture, whisking constantly, until it thickens and reaches 170°F (77°C) on a thermometer. This should take about 8-10 minutes.
3. **Add Butter:**
    - Remove the bowl from the heat and whisk in the butter, one piece at a time, until fully melted and combined. Stir in a pinch of salt.
4. **Cool:**
    - Strain the curd through a fine-mesh sieve into a clean bowl to remove any curdled bits. Let it cool to room temperature, then refrigerate until ready to use.

Assemble the Tarts:

1. **Fill the Tart Shells:**
    - Spoon or pipe the cooled key lime curd into the prepared tart shells, smoothing the tops.
2. **Chill:**
    - Refrigerate the tarts for at least 2 hours to allow the curd to set and firm up.
3. **Serve:**
    - Garnish with whipped cream, lime zest, or fresh berries if desired. Serve chilled.

Tips:

- **Zesting:** Be sure to zest the limes before juicing them to get the most flavor.
- **Texture:** The key lime curd should be smooth and creamy. If it seems too thick, you can whisk in a bit more lime juice before cooling.
- **Decorating:** For an extra touch, you can use a piping bag to add decorative dollops of whipped cream on top of the tarts.

Key Lime Curd Tarts are a refreshing and elegant dessert with a perfect blend of tart and sweet. Enjoy these delightful tarts as a special treat for any occasion!

Tropical Avocado and Mango Salad

Ingredients:

- **1 ripe avocado** (peeled, pitted, and diced)
- **1 ripe mango** (peeled, pitted, and diced)
- **1 small red bell pepper** (diced)
- **1/4 cup red onion** (finely chopped)
- **1/4 cup fresh cilantro** (chopped)
- **1/2 cup cherry tomatoes** (halved)
- **1 tablespoon olive oil**
- **1 tablespoon freshly squeezed lime juice** (about 1 lime)
- **1 teaspoon honey** (or to taste)
- **Salt and black pepper** (to taste)
- **Optional: 1/4 cup crumbled feta cheese** (for added flavor)

Instructions:

1. **Prepare the Ingredients:**
   - Dice the avocado and mango into bite-sized pieces. Dice the red bell pepper and finely chop the red onion. Halve the cherry tomatoes.
2. **Combine the Vegetables and Fruit:**
   - In a large bowl, gently toss together the diced avocado, mango, red bell pepper, cherry tomatoes, and red onion.
3. **Make the Dressing:**
   - In a small bowl or jar, whisk together the olive oil, lime juice, honey, salt, and black pepper. Adjust the seasoning to taste.
4. **Toss the Salad:**
   - Pour the dressing over the salad and gently toss to combine, ensuring the dressing coats all the ingredients evenly.
5. **Add Fresh Herbs:**
   - Gently fold in the chopped fresh cilantro.
6. **Optional: Add Feta Cheese:**
   - If using feta cheese, sprinkle it over the salad just before serving.
7. **Serve:**
   - Serve the salad immediately for the freshest taste, or chill it in the refrigerator for about 30 minutes before serving to let the flavors meld.

Tips:

- **Ripeness:** Ensure the avocado and mango are ripe but still firm to avoid mushiness.
- **Variations:** Add other tropical fruits like pineapple or papaya for extra flavor. You can also include sliced radishes or cucumbers for added crunch.
- **Dressing:** Adjust the sweetness of the dressing by adding more or less honey based on your preference.

Tropical Avocado and Mango Salad is a colorful, nutrient-packed dish that's bursting with tropical flavors. It's perfect for warm weather or anytime you want a taste of the tropics!

Coconut Macadamia Nut Cookies

Ingredients:

- **1 cup unsalted butter** (softened, at room temperature)
- **1 cup granulated sugar**
- **1 cup packed brown sugar**
- **2 large eggs**
- **1 teaspoon vanilla extract**
- **3 cups all-purpose flour**
- **1 teaspoon baking powder**
- **1/2 teaspoon baking soda**
- **1/2 teaspoon salt**
- **1 1/2 cups shredded sweetened coconut**
- **1 cup macadamia nuts** (chopped)

Instructions:

1. **Preheat the Oven:**
   - Preheat your oven to 350°F (175°C). Line baking sheets with parchment paper or silicone baking mats.
2. **Prepare the Dough:**
   - In a large bowl, cream together the softened butter, granulated sugar, and brown sugar until light and fluffy.
   - Beat in the eggs one at a time, then mix in the vanilla extract.
3. **Combine Dry Ingredients:**
   - In a separate bowl, whisk together the flour, baking powder, baking soda, and salt.
4. **Mix Dry and Wet Ingredients:**
   - Gradually add the dry ingredients to the butter mixture, mixing just until combined.
5. **Add Coconut and Macadamia Nuts:**
   - Gently fold in the shredded coconut and chopped macadamia nuts until evenly distributed throughout the dough.
6. **Scoop the Dough:**
   - Use a cookie scoop or tablespoon to drop rounded balls of dough onto the prepared baking sheets, spacing them about 2 inches apart.
7. **Bake:**
   - Bake for 10-12 minutes, or until the edges are golden brown but the centers are still soft.
8. **Cool:**
   - Allow the cookies to cool on the baking sheets for about 5 minutes before transferring them to wire racks to cool completely.

Tips:

- **Butter:** Make sure the butter is softened to room temperature to ensure a smooth, creamy dough.
- **Coconut:** You can use either sweetened or unsweetened shredded coconut depending on your preference.
- **Macadamia Nuts:** For a more intense nut flavor, lightly toast the macadamia nuts before chopping and adding them to the dough.
- **Consistency:** The cookies will continue to firm up as they cool, so be careful not to overbake them.

Coconut Macadamia Nut Cookies are a delightful combination of chewy, nutty, and tropical flavors that are sure to please any cookie lover. Enjoy these treats with a cup of tea or coffee, or simply on their own!

Caribbean Curried Chicken

Ingredients:

- **2 lbs chicken thighs or drumsticks** (skinless and bone-in)
- **2 tablespoons vegetable oil** (or coconut oil)
- **1 large onion** (chopped)
- **3 cloves garlic** (minced)
- **1 tablespoon fresh ginger** (grated)
- **2 tablespoons curry powder** (preferably Caribbean curry powder)
- **1 teaspoon allspice**
- **1/2 teaspoon paprika**
- **1/2 teaspoon turmeric**
- **1/2 teaspoon cayenne pepper** (adjust to taste)
- **1 large bell pepper** (diced)
- **2 medium tomatoes** (diced)
- **1 cup coconut milk**
- **1 cup chicken broth**
- **1-2 tablespoons brown sugar** (optional, to taste)
- **Salt and black pepper** (to taste)
- **1-2 sprigs fresh thyme** (or 1 teaspoon dried thyme)
- **2 tablespoons chopped fresh cilantro** (for garnish)

Instructions:

1. **Prepare the Chicken:**
   - Season the chicken pieces with salt and black pepper.
2. **Sear the Chicken:**
   - Heat the vegetable oil in a large pot or Dutch oven over medium-high heat. Add the chicken pieces and sear until browned on all sides. Remove the chicken and set aside.
3. **Cook the Aromatics:**
   - In the same pot, add the chopped onion and cook until softened, about 5 minutes. Add the garlic and ginger and cook for an additional 1-2 minutes, until fragrant.
4. **Add Spices:**
   - Stir in the curry powder, allspice, paprika, turmeric, and cayenne pepper. Cook for 1 minute to toast the spices.
5. **Add Vegetables:**
   - Add the diced bell pepper and tomatoes. Cook for 3-4 minutes, allowing the vegetables to soften.
6. **Simmer the Chicken:**
   - Return the seared chicken to the pot. Pour in the coconut milk and chicken broth, and stir to combine. Add the brown sugar (if using) and thyme.
7. **Cook:**

       - Bring the mixture to a simmer. Reduce the heat to low, cover, and cook for 30-40 minutes, or until the chicken is cooked through and tender.
8. **Adjust Seasoning:**
       - Taste and adjust seasoning with additional salt, pepper, or brown sugar if needed.
9. **Garnish and Serve:**
       - Garnish with chopped fresh cilantro before serving.

Tips:

- **Spice Level:** Adjust the cayenne pepper according to your preferred level of heat.
- **Coconut Milk:** Full-fat coconut milk will give the sauce a richer texture, but light coconut milk can be used for a lighter version.
- **Serving Suggestions:** Serve the curried chicken over rice, with roti, or alongside a fresh salad.

Caribbean Curried Chicken is a delightful, flavorful dish that brings a taste of the tropics to your table. Enjoy the aromatic spices and tender chicken in this savory and satisfying meal!

Grilled Banana with Rum Sauce

Ingredients:

For the Grilled Bananas:

- **4 ripe bananas** (peeled and cut in half lengthwise)
- **2 tablespoons unsalted butter** (melted)
- **1 tablespoon brown sugar**

For the Rum Sauce:

- **1/4 cup unsalted butter**
- **1/4 cup brown sugar**
- **2 tablespoons dark rum** (or light rum, if preferred)
- **1/4 cup heavy cream**
- **Pinch of salt**
- **Optional: 1/2 teaspoon vanilla extract**

Instructions:

1. **Prepare the Bananas:**
   - Preheat your grill to medium-high heat.
   - Brush the cut sides of the bananas with melted butter and sprinkle with brown sugar.
2. **Grill the Bananas:**
   - Place the bananas cut-side down on the grill. Grill for about 2-3 minutes, or until you see nice grill marks and the bananas are slightly softened.
   - Flip the bananas and grill for an additional 1-2 minutes on the other side, until heated through and caramelized.
3. **Make the Rum Sauce:**
   - In a medium saucepan over medium heat, melt the butter.
   - Stir in the brown sugar and cook until the sugar is dissolved and the mixture starts to bubble, about 2-3 minutes.
   - Carefully add the rum (it may flame up briefly) and stir to combine. Allow the rum to cook off for about 1 minute.
   - Reduce the heat to low and stir in the heavy cream. Simmer for 2-3 minutes, until the sauce has thickened slightly. Add a pinch of salt and vanilla extract if using.
4. **Serve:**
   - Place the grilled bananas on serving plates. Spoon the warm rum sauce over the bananas.
5. **Garnish:**
   - Optionally, garnish with a scoop of vanilla ice cream, a sprinkle of toasted coconut, or a few fresh mint leaves.

Tips:

- **Banana Ripeness:** Use ripe bananas for natural sweetness and a softer texture. Avoid overripe bananas as they might become too mushy on the grill.
- **Grill Temperature:** Make sure the grill is preheated to medium-high for the best caramelization of the bananas.
- **Rum Safety:** Be cautious when adding rum to the hot pan, as it can ignite briefly. Ensure the alcohol is cooked off to avoid a strong alcohol flavor.

Grilled Banana with Rum Sauce is a sumptuous dessert that brings together the smoky sweetness of grilled bananas with a luxurious rum sauce. It's perfect for a summer barbecue or any time you want to enjoy a tropical treat!

Pineapple Coconut Muffins

Ingredients:

- 1 1/2 cups all-purpose flour
- 1 cup granulated sugar
- 1 teaspoon baking powder
- 1/2 teaspoon baking soda
- 1/2 teaspoon salt
- 1/2 cup unsweetened shredded coconut
- 1/2 cup crushed pineapple (drained)
- 1/2 cup unsalted butter (melted)
- 2 large eggs
- 1/2 cup plain Greek yogurt (or sour cream)
- 1 teaspoon vanilla extract

Optional Glaze:

- 1/2 cup powdered sugar
- 1-2 tablespoons pineapple juice (or milk)

Instructions:

1. **Preheat the Oven:**
   - Preheat your oven to 350°F (175°C). Line a muffin tin with paper liners or lightly grease it.
2. **Prepare Dry Ingredients:**
   - In a large bowl, whisk together the flour, granulated sugar, baking powder, baking soda, salt, and shredded coconut.
3. **Combine Wet Ingredients:**
   - In another bowl, mix the melted butter, eggs, Greek yogurt (or sour cream), and vanilla extract until well combined.
4. **Add Pineapple:**
   - Gently fold in the crushed pineapple into the wet mixture.
5. **Combine Wet and Dry Ingredients:**
   - Add the wet ingredients to the dry ingredients and mix until just combined. Do not overmix; the batter should be slightly lumpy.
6. **Fill Muffin Tin:**
   - Divide the batter evenly among the muffin cups, filling each about 2/3 full.
7. **Bake:**
   - Bake for 18-22 minutes, or until a toothpick inserted into the center of a muffin comes out clean.
8. **Cool:**
   - Allow the muffins to cool in the pan for about 5 minutes, then transfer them to a wire rack to cool completely.

9. **Optional Glaze:**
   - If using the glaze, mix the powdered sugar with enough pineapple juice (or milk) to reach a drizzling consistency. Drizzle over the cooled muffins.

Tips:

- **Pineapple:** Make sure to drain the crushed pineapple well to prevent the muffins from becoming too wet.
- **Coconut:** For an extra coconut flavor, you can use toasted shredded coconut or add a handful of coconut flakes to the batter.
- **Storage:** Store the muffins in an airtight container at room temperature for up to 3 days, or freeze for longer storage.

Pineapple Coconut Muffins are a delightful way to enjoy tropical flavors in a convenient and delicious form. They're perfect for adding a touch of sunshine to your day!